BUILDING A TOTAL QUALITY CULTURE

By
Joe Batten

Crisp Publications, Inc.
Menlo Park, California

BUILDING A TOTAL QUALITY CULTURE

by Joe Batten

Copyright © 1992 by Joe Batten
Printed in the United States of America

Crisp Publications, Inc.
Menlo Park, California

Library of Congress Catalog Card Number 92-54371
Batten, Joe
Building A Total Quality Culture
ISBN 1-56052-176-7

Gimmicks, nostrums, quick fixes, and one-minute solutions abound. This book presents an approach that systematically designs and builds a culture in which a total emphasis on quality reaches and affects all policies, practices, processes, and people.

All the creative breakthroughs in quality must originate with people. The people you want in your organization, regardless of position, want to grow in personal and group leadership skills. They want to be led, not driven.

This book provides a comprehensive menu for people who want to function fully as individuals and who want to work in fully functioning organizations where self-led teams proliferate and vision-led individuals abound.

When the insights and tools provided here are blended into a purposeful and focused life and leadership style, quantum leaps in quality will occur.

Even though the strategy of zero defects is gaining popularity, it is crucial to focus on the fact that "zero defects" is essentially *defensive* and focuses on what *shouldn't* happen. Simply preventing defects is a small part of what organizations of the future must target and tool for. New, creative, and different methods of responding to a *customer-led* culture, one wherein wants, needs, and possibilities sensitively are sought and acted upon is the wave of tomorrow.

Above all, tough-minded TQC leaders are committed to:

Continuous Improvement!

Continuous Improvement!!

Continuous Improvement!!!

Will you do it?

Acknowledgments _____

Everything I create or publish is ably aided and stimulated by a great team. On the home front my thanks go to my wife, Jean, daughters Gail and Wendy and son-in-law Mark Havemann. I am indeed blessed.

For over 35 years my professional colleagues and their splendid contributions have been too numerous to mention. They have brought experiences from hundred of clients throughout the world to our creative sessions. Their commitment to total quality is manifest.

Associates who made significant and specific contributions to this particular book are Leonard Hudson, friend and colleague for over 40 years, Melva Edwards, my Executive Assistant, and gifted stalwarts like Bill Pearce, Jared Van Horn, Chris Hudson, and Norm Fleming. They are often my mentors as well as mentees.

Other gifted professionals include Ross Perot, Berkley Bedell, George Morrisey, Robert Randolph, John Teets, Jack Twyman, Don Kirkpatrick, Zig Ziglar, and Donald Alstadt.

Finally, our clients. They provided challenges, opportunities, and feedback that were invaluable.

This book is dedicated to Leonard Hudson.

Foreword _____

Intellectually challenging, emotionally stimulating, ethically and pragmatically sound, *Building a Total Quality Culture* gives us more than food for thought. It gives us a roadmap to follow in a time when leadership, quality, and performance are much-needed and in short supply.

A wise man once said that truth can be denied but it cannot be avoided. Joe Batten is a subscriber to that concept. He doesn't always write the things we would like to read, but he does write the things we need to read and he writes them in a manner which makes us not only willing to read them but to take action as well. Joe believes that leadership and management are the essential ingredients in the dough that will enable you—*and* your business—to perform better and rise higher in the intensely competitive world of today and tomorrow.

He offers very few clichés and no easy solutions, but he gives us all that marvelous ingredient called "hope," because his approach has believability. He does this by taking old-fashioned principles and adding modern technology and procedures which he skillfully blends together.

Dwight Eisenhower once said that leadership is the ability to persuade others to do what you want them to do because they want to do it. Two additional thoughts: Without integrity you will be unable to persuade a person to do what you want them to do because without integrity no one listens and without trust no one follows. In any endeavor in life it's true that you must be before you can do and you've got to do before you can have. You must be the right kind of person before you can be the right kind of leader. *Building a Total Quality Culture* challenges and teaches you how to "be" and do.

Because of Joe Batten's integrity and considerable experience as a leadership and management authority, and because what he does is consistent with what he says, this new book brings complete credibility and hence effectiveness to the marketplace. Joe Batten blends the theory of academia with the practicality of successful real-life experiences in his personal, family and business life. This approach gives credibility to the ideas, concepts, procedures, and integrity he teaches.

As you read *Building a Total Quality Culture* you get the distinct feeling that Joe Batten not only loves what he's doing and believes in the principles he's advocating, but that he genuinely wants you to be the beneficiary of his research, expertise, and many years of successful experience. He writes from both his head and his heart, and from a rich background of success. He knows what he's talking about, believes in what he's talking about, and communicates that your best interest is what he has at heart. He says a great deal in a very compact volume. His research is extensive, his documentation is thorough, his message is significant, and through it all hope prevails because his expertise and integrity make it completely believable. *Good stuff.*

Zig Ziglar

About This Book

FUNDAMENTAL PRINCIPLES FOR BUILDING
A TOTAL QUALITY CULTURE

- All people are walking bundles of strengths. "Weaknesses" are simply insufficiently developed strengths.

- Everyone needs clear feelings of purpose, direction, and expectation.

- Everyone has a deep need to feel significant and unique—the stuff of real dignity.

- One should, above all, expect the best from every dimension of life. A quality inner life leads to a rich and abundant total life.

- An open and tough mind grows. A closed and rigid mind dies.

- A tough-minded leader provides a transcendent or macro-vision and a magnetic lift and pull like a compass. This kind of leader provides purpose and direction.

- A tough-minded leader provides a crystal-clear focus of all of an organization's strengths.

- A tough-minded leader is committed to people, service, innovation, and quality. Such commitment is liberating and enriching to everyone in an organization.

- A tough-minded leader leads by example—by being focused and positive, and by stretching. A tough-minded leader is motive-led and value-fed.

- A tough-minded leader expects total integrity and ensures that all compensation is related to positive performance. All decisions are guided by these two components.

Contents _____

Preface   *iii*

Acknowledgments   *iv*

Foreword   *v*

About This Book   *vii*

Chapter 1: **The Path to the Future**   1

Chapter 2: **The New Leaders**   13

Chapter 3: **Making Quality Possibilites Come True**   25

Chapter 4: **Peak Performance at All Levels**   39

Chapter 5: **Winners Can Be Grown**   51

Chapter 6: **Tomorrow's Culture**   63

              Bibliography   73

              Glossary   75

Chapter 1 _____

The Path to the Future

Empowerment involves the sense people have that they are at the center of things.

—Warren Bennis,
Executive Excellence,
April, 1992

The predominant role of the Total Quality Culture (TQC) leader is to have visions and dreams, to define an organization's mission, and to identify its superordinate goals—to discipline the path to the future.

Enthused, energetic, but somewhat befogged executives across America are asking, "What's visioneering? What's the definition or difference between a vision, a mission, a dream? A transcendent or superordinate goal? Where do personal values and philosophy fit in?"

Since we all ultimately become what we think, say and do, it is crucial to understand these terms, particularly "visioneering." A *vision* is the situation we see in our mind. We visualize the macro results we want to achieve. A *mission* is a generally targeted and focused statement of intended macro results; it is the basis for more specific goals and expectations. A *dream* is a deeply felt and yearned-for hope of the possible, but without specific intent.

A *philosophy* is usually a relatively comprehensive body of truths, values and beliefs that fuel, fuse and focus the genesis of the *dream,* the stimulation of the *vision,* and the formulation of the *mission.*

These transcendent feelings and statements are the major responsibility and commitments of true leaders. To lead, we must evocatively pull our team members toward macro commitments that are larger than ourselves. We must elicit, free up, and liberate. We must empower.

In the absence of a vision there can be no clear and consistent focus. In the absence of a dream there can be no renewal of hope. In the absence of a philosophy there is no real meaning in work and in life itself.

The opposite of the Total Quality Culture leader who walks in front of the flock is the all-too-common "driver" who walks behind the flock. This person is not a leader at all, but rather a pusher or driver who compresses, represses and depresses. These obsolete managers tend to use phrases like "value-driven," "market-driven," and "data-driven," *ad infinitum, ad nauseam.*

The true TQC leader believes in, exemplifies, and teaches the concepts of value-led, market-led, and data-led.

How can one be enthusiastic about a vision or dream and then perpetuate an organizational culture in which people and things are driven? Leading, pulling, stretching, reaching and striving upward and onward are the marks of the visioneer.

THE VALUE-LED VISIONEER

Visioneering leaders manage as though they had no rank, as though they had to depend totally on the quality of the ideas that they express daily by their own examples. The new TQC leader's arsenal of values contains a rich variety of beliefs:

- *Information is the ultimate resource.* It is the stuff of all human interaction.

- *Change is the only constant in the world.* Winners live in a state of flow and thrive on change. Losers always look for static stability. To have vitality, there must be change.

- *The leader is in; the driver is out.* Stretching stimulates growth; pushing compresses and deadens. People cannot be supervised or "directed" into excellence — they must be led and stretched.

- *Winners can be grown.* The value you contribute is the sum of your values. The yeast in the culture (corporate or otherwise) determines what grows.

- *Leaders can learn to plan while in motion.* We must move from mental rigidity to mental suppleness and agility (thus creating mental toughness).

- *Ethical management pays off.* A clear conscience creates good mental hygiene. Integrity is strength.

- *Visioneers stop telling, commanding, and coercing: instead, they ask, listen, and hear.* Above all, leaders build on people's strengths. Visualize each person as a bundle of strengths. Speak to, listen to, and hear those strengths. Think of weaknesses as the absence of strengths or as insufficiently developed strengths.

- *TQC visioneers are person-centered rather than role-centered.*

- *Tough-minded visioneers thrive on **quality** nutrients* such as confidence, self-respect, courage, commitment, integrity, stretch, moral values, resilience, tenacity, mental agility. sensitiveness to change, openness, emotional vulnerability, and a belief in something or someone greater than the self.

- *A personal feeling of significance is the ultimate human need.* Empowered people believe that what they do is significant and meaningful. When they are empowered, people see themselves as at the center of things; they feel that they are valued.

- *Clearly stated expectations that stretch people enhance their feelings of significance.*

- *Peak performers are motivated by a passionate commitment to a transcendent vision, dream, or mission.* Winners and losers alike carry a toolbox with them. The tools, however, are different. Winners' tools are expectational; losers' tools are directive.

- *Responsiveness is the key to all unusual success stories.* Organizations that fail to respond dynamically will become mediocre at best.

- *High-tech/high-touch will steadily evolve toward high-touch/high-tech.* Human factors must have priority at all times.

- *Peak-performing organizations and individuals are value-led rather than value-driven.* They are customer-led rather than customer-driven. This will be one of the most dramatic new developments in management and leadership.

- *All real management is self-management*—the new ideal.

- *The new buzzwords* include vision, creativity, responsiveness, internal entrepreneuring, conceptual thinking, innovation, pro-activity, integrity, mental agility, morals, values, and reorientation.

- *Change can frighten, depress, and paralyze, or it can challenge, stretch, and enrich.*

- *Applied possibility thinking and "possibility teams" will grow steadily.* New and creative kinds of team building will be crucial and will flourish in the 1990s.

- *Qualified "quality consultants" will be in short supply and will be able to name their fees.*

- *The most practical thing in the world is applied thought.*

- *The epigram "Work is love made visible," will take on new meaning and relevance in the workplace.*

- *Enlightened visioneers recognize that human effort can and must be focused like a laser beam.* Ralph Waldo Emerson said "Concentration is the source of strength in politics, in war, in trade, in short, in all the management of human affairs."

Our value is the sum of our values. In the absence of these conceptual conditions—or in the absence of a lean, clean, dynamic blend—there is no stretch, pull, reaching or stimulus to move forward.

A TOTAL QUALITY CULTURE:

Revaluing American Organizations

American organizations are being studied with unprecedented intensity, in an effort to help our businesses move back into the vanguard in the world arena. Academic and corporate soothsayers are saying—often simplistically—that the solution is TQM, or total quality management.

This would be great if the concepts and tactics for this renaissance were properly reasoned and practiced. However, inanimate processes and procedures are often stressed while human dynamics, are neglected. What is needed is an enlightened understanding of the kind of leadership needed to compellingly fuse and focus the strengths of all of the *people* in the organization on quality goals that stretch them.

Statistics, processes, and technology are great as far as they go—but they don't go nearly far enough.

FOCUS ON VALUES

The total value of an organization is the sum of the values it promotes, teaches, and practices.

The United States has been a world leader because of its values. Only values can motivate people to work effectively. Values held in common compel the people in an organization to focus their energies on excelling in a common purpose. Only by reemphasizing those common values can we be in the vanguard in the world arena. Leadership can only be effective when it exemplifies the highest vision and values.

The total quality of an organization is the sum of its actualized leadership qualities in action . . . and the products that result. Already we are beginning to see organizations that are discovering that, while sophisticated statistical processes are essential, they are not enough. My colleagues and I feel a deep concern, because there is a lack of a 1990s approach to quality leadership; this lack is serious and must have immediate attention. We must shift our emphasis. Managers manage things. Leaders lead *people!*

If you envision the corporation as an organic whole, complete with circulatory, respiratory, and neural systems, you can easily see that a statistical or quantitative treatment deals only with the skeleton of the organization. We must go way beyond this to create a fully functioning, 'beyond-quality' culture or corporate *being.*

Culture in a business is "the things we believe in and the way we do them here." The culture should be founded on carefully researched, designed, and communicated philosophy, on a statement of beliefs and values, on a transcendent set of goals—a vision.

It's people, not statistical analyses, that transform a vision into reality. The people culture, properly conceived and executed, optimizes the leadership abilities of employees. Ross Perot, when asked about the success of EDS, said, "I love the members of my team!" Perot expected everybody on the payroll to be trained as leaders, and treated as leaders, and expected them to lead.

NEW PARADIGMS

We must constantly, responsively, and incessantly challenge all existing paradigms. The Total Quality Culture (TQC) organization of the 1990s is *value-centered* and *value-led.* TQC-focused executives who are TMLs (Tough-Minded Leaders) lead and pull team members toward the practice of a comprehensive battery of new paradigms. Your team—indeed your entire organization—can learn and adopt this new culture as their own. Key TQC cultural components include:

- Commitment to transcendent vision, missions and goals.

- Recognizing that people will follow *learners.* They will not follow *knowers.*

- Targeting the creative and logical deployment of people's strengths as the organization principle of the future.

- Continually translating values into action.

- Placing a premium on the *team* at all times.

- Fostering and training self-led teams.

- Promoting passionate rather than passive behavior.

- Targeting results that pull, not push.

- Providing dynamic autonomy, delegation and empowerment.

- Fostering the shared belief that "we can accomplish anything: the difficult we do immediately, the impossible takes a little longer."

- Personal leadership that others want to emulate and follow. Leadership is simply not possible without people who are willing to follow.

- Rewarding learners rather than knowers.

- A pervasive culture of commitment to continuous learning and to new dimensions of service.

- Understanding and practicing leadership at *every* level and *every* part of the organization.

- Creating job evaluation criteria based on innovation, quality, creativity, and change. Performance is all that matters!

- Creating policies and programs that build and enhance a high level of physical, mental, and spiritual energy.

- Stretching and clarifying all dimensions of the culture.

- Giving *earned* praise freely. Don't stint!

Daily exposure to one or more of these statements can change attitudes throughout the organization.

ATTITUDE IS EVERYTHING

Attitudes are the mental and emotional manifestations of our values. Empowered team members feel valuable and become capable of a much better quality of workmanship than those who feel powerless, vague, confused, negative, or overtly or covertly hostile. Paradigm shifts for the 1990s must focus with monomaniacal intensity on empowering the individual and the team — which, of course, are indivisible!

Strong, empowered teams are the products of the individual strengths of team members who are strength-oriented, focused, and reinforced, and who are very clear about expectations for their performance.

Team members commit to unusually high levels of quality only when and if they thoroughly understand *why*. A fuzzy understanding of the task and quality goals leads to uncertain quality results.

Expect The Best

Believe that there are strengths, possibilities, and latent richness in all situations, people and events.

Provide unusual and unparalleled service.

Incessantly seek knowledge and growth.

LAUNCHING THE TQC

When key executives ask, "Okay, what do we do to get under way on this? We recommend a seven-phase process:

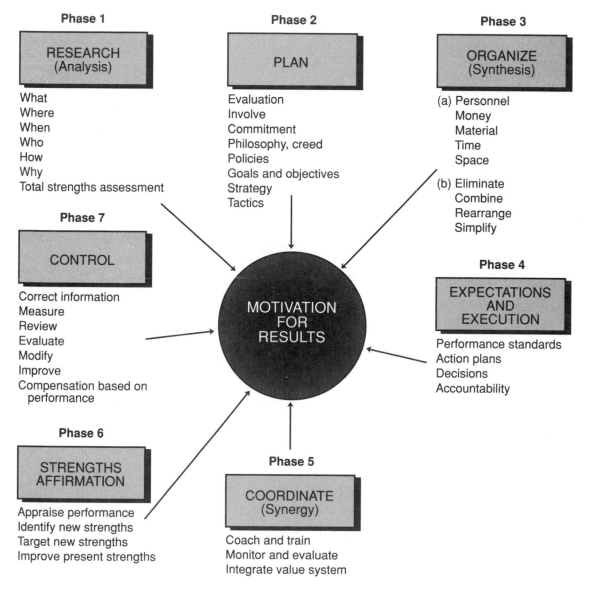

FIGURE 1.

THE NEW QUALITY CULTURE

My colleagues and I have done consulting and training work in hundreds of companies ranging from Fortune 500 giants to very small, entrepreneurial companies. We have verified over and over again the lessons of history—that purely directive or coercive power is elusive and ephemeral. Military power, economic power, jurisdictional and political power can crumble quickly. Mental power alone endures. It demands change, quality, growth and forward movement. If you want to change organizational habits, change the people. If you want to change people, make sure that the right nutrients are provided for their minds.

The Total Quality Culture (TQC) develops a working system for idea optimization. The single most crucial and effective form of power for the turbulent decades ahead is the power of ideas expressed by example and implemented in a system of clear, focused expectations. Only this power can prevail and optimize the humanity of people in an age in which technology is too often given priority over people. Technology is a human product.

The lessons for the culture of the future are clear: vision, values, innovation, renewal, quality, commitment, energy, discipline and personal leadership can build a great and exciting tomorrow. Truly discerning leaders know that compressed, pushed, driven people simply cannot and will not produce outstanding quality. They must be led.

Attitude is everything. Our attitudes are a product of our experience, the information we ingest, the thoughts we think, the words we use, and the way other people respond to us. In global terms, we must raise our sights, loosen our biases, and let our minds go forth.

It's also crucial to be willing to set a goal so high that you risk failure. All great leaders have discovered the crucial necessity of failing forward.

Care enough to create a culture that reflects the pervasive empowerment of people—a streamlined culture that epitomizes service, quality, empowerment, innovation, vision, and values. Cultures are built either on a rock of proven principles or on the shifting sand of short-term expediency. Build a Total Quality Culture, and your company will stand the test of time.

LEADERSHIP NUTS AND BOLTS

(Fed and Led by Values)

At the center—and up front—of the Total Quality Culture is the new paradigm of Tough-Minded Leadership. The twelve principles that follow are the bare bones of this paradigm:

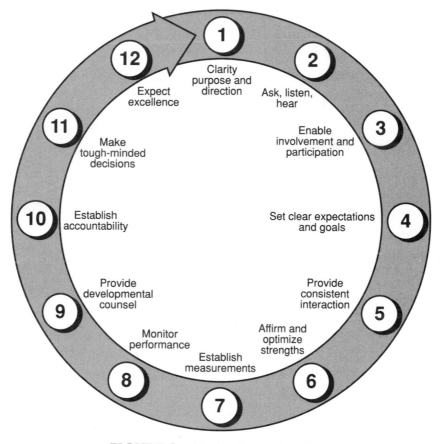

FIGURE 2. Twelve Principles of TML

If every member of your team makes a commitment to these twelve principles, imagine what you could achieve:

1. I will ensure that my organization, my team members, and I develop clear purpose and direction.

2. I will ask, listen to, and hear my colleagues, to best understand and use their strengths.

3. I will ensure that they feel a sense of involvement, participation, and identification with our goals and objectives.

4. I will ensure that all members of the team know clearly what results—expectations—justify their place in the organization.

5. I will provide consistent information and encourage sharing and coordination.

6. I will affirm and optimize team members' strengths.

7. I will ensure that specific qualitative and quantitative performance indicators are developed.

8. I will ensure that I receive and provide lean, clean and timely progress reports in order to monitor the team's performance.

9. I will ensure that each member of my team is provided with excellent counsel to optimize growth and performance.

10. I will establish both the mechanics and dynamics needed to reward performance or correct failure.

11. I will make decisions and solve problems when and where circumstances require.

12. I will expect the best from myself and my team at all times.

Rigorously avoid rationalizing poor results or blaming the Japanese and competing with them. Using TQC principles, compete with your own internally generated objectives, goals, and possibilities! Who is more challenging to compete with than ourselves? Motorola and Harley-Davidson are excellent examples of how this can work. Above all, demonstrate tough-minded resolve and *act*.

MENTAL TOUGHNESS

> *If vision is the essence of being a coach, then mental toughness is the one quality a coach must possess. Vision without mental toughness is nothing more than a good idea.*
>
> —Vincent H. Lombardi
> *Executive Excellence*
> April, 1992

Chapter 2

The New Leaders

Mindsets are yesterday — mind growth is tomorrow.

—Joe Batten

New cultures *can* only be forged from new attitudes, tough-minded action, and the *elusive art of excellent leadership.*

How can we create new TQC leadership for the decade ahead? How can we develop a new breed of renaissance leaders? Reading about a new philosophy is not enough. Reciting slogans such as "We're committed to excellence" won't do it. Sending managers to seminars, workshops, and courses won't do it, either. These actions can help, but much more is required.

Real change elements can be categorized under three headings: attitude, action, and art.

ATTITUDE

The precursor of all change in every dimension of our lives is attitude. When attitudes are expressed through centered, focused action, and action is nurtured and guided at all times by a vision of the *art* of leadership, change occurs.

Leadership is too often taught and practiced at the level of craft or profession. That may work for the short term, but to achieve TQC, leaders must practice leadership at the level of art. Passivity is out; passion is in!

Intuitive, artful TQC leaders constantly and relentlessly move from the attitudes of the past to the attitudes of the future. Some of these key changes are:

From	To
High-tech/high-touch	High-touch/high-tech
Product primacy	Customer primacy
Value-driven	Value-led
Customer-driven	Customer-led
Employee-driven	Team member-led
Analysis of weaknesses	Evaluation of strengths
Fuzzy, arbitrary directives	Clear, flexible expectations
Driving, compressing, depressing	Leading, stretching, resilient
Passive mental rigidity	Passionate suppleness
Telling	Asking
Expedient policies	Deep ethical commitment
Dissatisfaction	Unsatisfaction
Dwelling on weaknesses	Building on Strengths
Provincial strategy and tactics	Global strategy and tactics

The value of people is the sum of their values, the tool box that is between the ears, the fire in their bellies. Concentrate with superbly centered energy on the values that comprise the attitudes that fuel the action that in turn stimulates the growth and quality of the art.

It has become fashionable to say, "We're committed to excellence of service" and to plaster these slogans on walls, desks, and corporate bumpers. But in most companies, these statements of intent don't produce any significant improvement in service to the customer because the insights and skills needed to actually achieve excellence are neglected or ignored. A quality culture must be pervasive.

Inner Space

Simply calling for change is not enough! I am attempting to redefine leadership so that trendy terms like human capital, flex-systems, vision, culture, empowerment, adaptation, skunkworks, innovation, and entrepreneurism can become reality. To accomplish this, we must achieve some profound changes in inner space—the space between the ears.

While I am as intrigued as any professional management practitioner by global trends so ably chronicled in many current books, the fact is that we can tool for competition and implement these sparkling new strategies only if we first accomplish profound changes in our insights, motives, confidence, and energy focus—and above all, in our values.

A gifted speaker recently told a group of members of Alcoholics Anonymous that alcohol was not the problem that created alcoholism. Rather, he said, it was the feelings of the people. The alcohol was incidental and expedient and then the addiction became a problem.

Just so with the leader/manager who is dissatisfied, troubled—even threatened—by the dire stories of competition by Japanese and other businesspeople throughout the world. The problem is not the competition. The problem, the challenge, is the person in the mirror. The problem, the opportunity, may be you.

Therefore, it is crucial for the new TQC leader to take a rigorous look at self and begin the renaissance at that point. We must start with ourselves.

ACTION

My experience is that top management simply cannot pervasively influence the culture, philosophy, principles, policies, processes, procedures, purpose, practices, people and profits without definitive attitudes, planned action, and artful persuasion.

Such actions entail carefully targeted and sequenced programs of:

Information dissemination
One-on-one mentoring and counseling
Imaginative creation of media instruments
Assignments and simulations
Workshops
Creative electronic mail
Clarity of expectations throughout the organization

Did Ross Perot content himself with platitudes about service? No, he initiated tough-minded methods of followthrough that affected every member of his team. He unceasingly expected their best.

In an interview in *Executive Excellence,* (April, 1986), Bill Marriott of the hotel empire provides insightful comments:

> Personal involvement in the details gives you the basis for planning. If you know your business, and you know what's going on out there, you can't be led along by strategists or theorists who don't know the real world you operate in.

> The competitive edge in this business is people. I'm trying to communicate that I care and that I think the role they play in the organization is an extremely vital one. I'm trying to remove fear. No manager can be fired unless he or she has been warned in writing three times. In performance reviews, we applaud strengths, pinpoint areas that need improvement, and determine (by asking, not telling) what assistance is needed.

When he was asked, "How do you manage to be fair and nice with people and yet demand excellence from them?" Marriott said: "Well, it's *tough-minded management,* which basically says that you treat people right and decent and fair and in return they give their all for you. We make sure they have the proper training to do a good job and they have what is required of them."

Closed, directive, rigid minds have no place in the toolbox of the new leaders. The hard, driving manager is out! The open, growing, changing, supple, and resilient-minded leader with high expectations is in! The executive of tomorrow will feel an ache, a lust, an insatiable need to change and grow.

In the splendid book *What Works for Me* by Thomas Horton, CEO of AMA, we find:

> The CEOs interviewed for this book are pulling their companies into the future. Possessing the will to decide, they are tough-minded, willing to live with their decisions, regardless of the results. While they insist on tough-mindedness in their people, they also hold themselves fully accountable. It is only through the actual practice of integrity that the valuable asset of trust can be forged and maintained.

The new leaders will be goal-oriented rather than role-oriented. They will possess vitality, values, vision and voltage. They will walk in front of the flock, rather than behind it.

THE ART OF LEADERSHIP

I advocate placing a premium on the *art* of leadership; on growing intuitive managers; on fostering innovation, creativity, and service; and on the capacity to relish change. But I must add that these delicious buzzwords will only remain grist for seminars until we focus relentlessly on the need to change basic attitudes; formulate lean, focused action plans; and move far beyond the "science" and "profession" of leadership and on to the elusive but enormously rewarding art of leadership.

I Challenge You

To those who yearn to truly lead and to commit to pervasive quality in the coming age of volatile change, I dare you:

- To dream big and put timetables in to that dream!
- To become all you can be and do all you can do!
- To shun rigidity by keeping an open but tough mind!
- To expect the best from yourself and others!
- To find something to love in every person!
- To set big goals and stretch to meet them!
- To fill your battery with faith, hope, love, and gratitude!
- To build (not destroy) with everything you think, say, and do!
- To live with a sense of wonder . . . a state of grace!
- To confront life openly and vulnerably with courage, faith, commitment, and confidence!
- To replace and displace loser attitudes by writing down 200 victories in your life since you were born!
- To create and build a personal strength notebook!
- To be an inspiring "go-*giver*"! (The go-*getter* ultimately gets got and forgot.)

In his book *The Frontiers of Management,* Peter Drucker says that what he advocated 30 years ago about the "spirit" of an organization is just now becoming understood in terms of "culture." The spirit of the organization is the voltage that charges and activates all else. Change can best be carried out when the elements of an organization's culture are the products of its spirit.

A true spirit of excellence, of innovation and creativity, can become reality much more quickly when the CEO's own example leads with such persuasion that people will *want* to hear what he or she says. It is not the documentable elements of strategy that the new CEO espouses, but rather his or her qualities that will guide the CEO as a person with positive ideas, dynamic action, and artful responses.

If you want to do inspiring research in leadership and management styles, study the personal vision, values, vitality and voltage of renaissance managers such as Ross Perot, Bill Marriott, Neil Springer of Navistar, Art Bauer of American Media, Bob Lookabaugh of Eye Max, and Jim Kimsey of Quantum Computer Systems. You will be able to see the substance—the tough-mindedness—behind the style.

A TOUGH-MINDED LEADERSHIP

Tough-minded leaders build on strengths rather than focus on weaknesses; they may also ask for sacrifices.

How long will we continue to confuse *management* with *leadership?* How long will the quick-fix approach to business success last? Will phrases like "how to swim with the sharks" and "the power of funkiness in business" endure?

Will we continue to provide MBA degrees that do not contain one course on the real nature and tools of leadership? Truly rugged individualism cannot be practiced by simply attempting to emulate the success story chronicled by management observers.

The true leader places a premium on mind-power—the power of self-generated ideas in action. The leader pulls rather than pushes; lifts rather than compresses, represses, or depresses.

Ross Perot has long endorsed *Tough-Minded Management* (Batten, 1963). Starting in 1964, he gave a copy of the book along with a handwritten note to every person who joined EDS; ultimately, all 45,000 EDS team members received a personal copy. The rest is history. Ross does not lay back and take his cues from other CEOs. He sets the pace, lifts and pulls.

To move beyond sterotyped notions of management to the crucial requirements of leadership requires major changes. Lean, clean, focused leadership—compasslike qualities—are critical characteristics for leaders of the future.

The competitive edge in all endeavors is people. Perhaps at no other time in history has the need for real leadership in all dimensions of our society been so acute. And leadership is of, by, about, and for people. Leadership is essentially a human business, and business is a product of leadership. In fact, CEOs all across the country agree that virtually every crisis of business is a crisis of leadership. Superb quality is a product of leadership.

Surprisingly, there is no clear, cogent, and consistent definition of leadership. Most books on leadership written in the last 30 years ignore the fact that one cannot lead unless one has followers. And no one can follow a pusher or a driver.

Pushers and drivers compress, repress and depress, deadening all initiative and individuality; they also fail to stimulate and inspire creativity and innovation.

Such managers tend to use phrases like "value-driven," "market-driven," and "data-driven." These are out-of-date concepts. The TQC leader believes in and teaches the concepts of value-led, market-led, data-led, and customer-led.

Warren Bennis and Burt Nanus write in their book *Leaders* (1985) that recognition and appreciation of self-worth is the most crucial requirement for leadership:

> Our study strongly suggested that a key factor in the executive's success was the creative deployment of self . . . our leaders do know their worth. . . .

> People without self-respect choke on self-reproach. Every unanswered letter becomes a monument to their own sloth, an epitaph to their guilt. Without self-respect, we give ourselves away and make the ultimate sacrifice. We sell ourselves out. The first step in achieving positive self-regard is recognizing strengths and compensating for weaknesses.

Their writing is based on a four-year study of 90 prominent achievers. Having worked with hundreds of leaders over the past 30 years, my colleagues and I agree fully with them.

Leader's Tool Kit

There is a kit of tools, an arsenal of values, for the person who wants to master the art of leadership. I believe such tools and values can be taught, mastered and practiced.

The first and greatest emphasis should be placed on recognizing and creatively deploying strengths. The total value—present and potential—of a person is the sum of the values he or she perceives and exemplifies. To focus and dwell on weaknesses is counterproductive, because it tends to polarize and rigidify the person's behavior and performance into a non-malleable, non-growth mold. We are the sum of our strengths! We are the sum of our expectations! And they are indivisible! Peak performers possessed of considerable ego strength are drawn toward performance that reflects excellence of quality.

The pragmatic, tough-minded TQC leader gives high priority to identifying, classifying, developing, deploying, and measuring strengths. The deepest need we have is for significance, and our feelings of significance grow in direct proportion to a growing awareness of our strengths as leaders and as total people.

The converse is also true. When we search for, dwell on, and reiterate the weaknesses of a person, we limit that person's possibilities, reduce their feelings of significance, inhibit growth on and off the job, and seriously hamper their performance. Second-rate quality is then inevitable. To overemphasize people's weaknesses is to saddle them with a miserable self-image. Work diligently, truthfully, and consistently to help your people understand, and use their strengths; it will set them free. Empowerment becomes more than a word.

Clear-eyed, objective, and consistent affirmation of strengths becomes one of the greatest pleasures for the committed—and highly expective—leader. He or she discovers that this adds zest to the job and to relationships with his or her family. TQC leaders understand that weaknesses should only be identified for the purpose of determining what additional strengths are needed or what is needed to further develop existing strengths.

The new maxim for tough-minded TQC leaders is this: Perhaps the finest gift one can give another is that of expecting to stretch themselves in a never-ending search for their present and potential strengths. Ken Blanchard has said, "Servant leadership is easy for people with high self-esteem. Such people have no problem giving credit to others, listening to other people for ideas, or building other people up."

True leadership thrives on an intense desire to serve. Socrates said, "Above all know thyself." Plato said, "Before we can move the world, we must first move ourselves." Christ said, "Follow me."

Abraham Lincoln attended church one Sunday and heard a well-known minister who many thought was at the peak of his form because the president of the United States was in his audience. When asked what he thought of the sermon, President Lincoln said, "Since you asked, I must confess I didn't think much of it." "Why?" he was asked. Lincoln replied, "Because he didn't ask us to do anything great."

Pulitzer Prize-winning historian James McGregor Burns, in his book *Leadership,* says "Transforming leaders *draw* people out of their narrow, material concerns; they often do so less by making promises to followers than by asking for sacrifice from them."

We need mentally tough leaders with vision, focus and action who spurn the G-forces that shackle us to the past and who embrace the lift and pull of the future. We need leaders who rigorously assess and change their appetites, passions, pride and pretensions, and ambitions. Tough-minded TQC leaders settle for nothing less!

Vincent H. Lombardi (son of the late Vince, Sr.) says: "Mental toughness can come in a 16-year-old, 84-pound package. You don't have to be a hulking middle linebacker to be tough."

LEADING BY EXPECTATION

The TQC leader who expects his or her people to perform their best achieves the greatest results. This is a central element of a new, emerging style of leadership.

It's a style of leadership that requires fundamental changes at a very deep level in management attitudes. Basically, it is this: *We become what we expect.* There is a direct link between what we expect from ourselves and our team members, and what we and they actually achieve in results that contribute directly to our company's quality and profits.

The majority of managers today still manage by directive. They tell, push, drive. They pigeonhole people into boxes on an organization chart. On the other hand, real leadership expects the best from each person and gives them goals they can stretch to reach. Most importantly, it holds them accountable for results, rewarding performance that contributes to corporate goals.

At the same time, TQC managers set the example by their own attitudes. They give people a model to follow. There is no separation between what he or she says and what he or she does.

To get the best results, you must do more than merely establish goals and objectives. You need to get your people involved in setting goals so they will make a commitment to them. They need to feel that the goals are *their* goals, not just the organization's goals. You must be willing to take the time to develop a real understanding of each of your team members' drives and ambitions.

Potent Laser

The difference between an ordinary room full of light and a potent laser beam is the degree of focus and intensity. This is a good metaphor for the difference between ordinary performance and the results that can be achieved where a team is committed to clearly stated goals.

Control does not come from the above. It is the self-control that comes from enlightened, involved, and committed people working together as a team with shared vision, wants, needs, and goals.

For many managers, it is easier to give orders than to develop people. The more indirect control that results from developing people needs managers with a certain "toughness"—a flexible, growing, stretching quality of mind. Expectations are far stronger than directives, and they achieve much greater results.

Consider two of the most profitable companies in the world: Motorola and the Tokyo-based Matsushita Industries, a Japanese electronics giant. Both are using TQC. Both build on strengths rather than focusing on weaknesses. They have discovered the tough-minded principle that our strengths are our tools. They have taken long steps toward a Total Quality Culture.

According to Thomas Watson, Jr. (1963), former chairman, IBM owes its success to the belief that "the basic philosophy, spirit, and drive of an organization have far more to do with its relative achievements than do technological or economic resources, organizational structure, innovation, and timing."

"Our most important belief," Watson states, "is our respect for the individual. This is a simple concept, but in IBM it occupies a major portion of management time. We devote more effort to it than anything else." IBM knows that management is of, by, about, and for people.

Konosuke Matsushita, founder of Matsushita Industries, told me: "There are many secrets of success, but the most important one, I think is looking for people's strong points and making the most of them. If I had only noticed their weak points, I would not have been able to ask anyone to work for me. There would then have been no working together." Matsushita referred to *Tough-Minded Management* as his "secular bible." I can almost hear the late Mr. Matsushita say, "Let us design and build a culture of quality."

Strong-Minded

It is important, then, to build on a person's strengths if we are to truly lead. All too often we judge people, pointing out all the things they do wrong. We should, in fact, evaluate them by searching for their strong points and helping them develop these. This does not mean that we ignore their areas of weakness. We acknowledge them but we do not focus all our attention on them.

The Total Quality Culture is affected by the belief that there are only two reasons for studying or examining weaknesses. They are to determine *what additional strengths are needed* and *what is needed to further develop one's present strengths.*

First, identify each person's strengths both existing and potential. (They are the only true tools and building units we possess.) Where can you use these strengths to help you achieve department, division, or company goals?

Then, when setting performance standards, challenge your people to meet stretching goals based on these strengths. And expect excellence from them. Hold them accountable for results, and reward them for the results they achieve.

Continuous feedback and compensation based on results foster a culture of self-control to improve performance. Be sure also to *give earned praise unstintingly.* If praise is earned, there is nothing more truly motivational. It also renews and recharges the one who does the praising.

Performance is based on people and improves only when people improve. Well-written performance standards are all expectations in concrete terms. They must define the results required, in terms that can be measured. And they must progressively provide more stretching goals to give people something to reach for.

As leaders, we have a choice: We can mold and compress a person to fit a job that has been carefully tied to other jobs, or we can encourage people to expand their capabilities and become part of a dynamically growing organization.

Do your people know exactly what you expect of them? Have you clearly defined policies and performance standards? Do your performance appraisals help them improve through constructive criticism and identification of strengths and areas for further training? We can drive or lead. We can compress, repress, and depress, or we can stretch, exemplify, and lead. While I question his use of the word "driven," I agree with Jack Welch, CEO of General Electric, when he says: "The world of the 90's and beyond will not belong to *managers* . . . the world will belong to passionate, driven *leaders*."

Solomon Said:

Without vision, the people perish.

The TQC Leader Says:

*Without leaders with vision —
a vision of a quality culture — total
quality is an illusion.*

Chapter 3

Making Quality Possibilities Come True

The key to success is to think long-term: to think in terms of building relationships and high-trust cultures.

—Steven R. Covey
Executive Excellence
April, 1992

From border to border and coast to coast—and beyond—I encounter these questions:

Where are the new frontiers?
What does *excellence* really mean?
How can I "exceed" myself?
How can I become truly creative?
What is real motivation all about?
What is real quality?

Some authorities seem to suggest that technology is what it is all about. I disagree emphatically! Technological breakthroughs are purely and simply of, by, about, and for the people. In turn, people are only as creative, effective, and happy as the *quality* of their minds.

The future clearly lies in the frontier—the space between the ears. A quality revolution on this frontier will be the sole source of better lives, better products and packaging, better human relationships, greater richness, and riches for total functioning as whole and growing organizational culture.

Considerable research clearly demonstrates that we barely begin to discover and use our full mental and spiritual possibilities in our lifetimes. Several years ago Alexander Solzhenitsyn said that the West was spiritually exhausted. What do you think?

Please reflect on these thoughts from the preface of my book, *Expectations and Possibilities.*

> Our attitudes are at the core of our being. They condition our biological anatomy, the activation of our brain cells, our choice of nutrition and exercise, and, ergo, the condition of our bodies. They condition our relationship with others. They are truly the agents of change and arbiters of the quality of our lives.
>
> Attitudes, then, are both our goal and our product. Excellence of attitudes is the beginning and the end—the alpha and omega.

Here is a Possibility Acronym that my colleagues and I have successfully used as consultants, mentors, and trainers in a wide variety of organizations. Please think deeply about each of the following in relation to your culture:

Positive, purposeful, and passionate
  Organization, openness, and opportunity
    Spirit and self-fulfillment
      Self-actualization
        Instrumentation of intrinsic strengths
          Believing, behaving, and becoming
            Investigate and install
              Love, light, and laughter
                Itinerary
                  Tactics and tempo
                    Insincerity
                      Excellence
                        Salubriousness

Let's look at this acronym for the possibility of winning more closely:

Positive, purposeful, and passionate.

When we focus our energies, actions, and tactics on a clearly discernible and stimulating purpose, we make optimum use of our time, energy, and personal tools. The lift and pull of a transcendent dream, carried out with passion, has been at the core of all breakthroughs in human progress and all great companies. Pasteur, Perot, Curie, Schweitzer, Thomas Watson, Peale, Emerson, Beethoven, Einstein, Iacocca, and many, many more who profoundly influenced their time, were all focused in such a way that they did not become vague, distracted, or caught up in self-doubt. Passion and passivity are used here to contrast the difference in the impact of those whose lives burn with the fires of great ideas and those who putter in a vague twilight of no goals. Passion lifts and enriches. Passivity dulls and deadens.

Organization, openness, and opportunity.

To capitalize on one's vision of what can be—of one's possibilities—we need the practical and effective blend of people, money, materials, time, and space. The intent is to create synergy—where the whole is greater than the sum of the parts. Synergy results when strengths are effectively deployed to capitalize on opportunities in a fast-moving, dynamic business world.

Openness is a crucial ingredient because we lose all growth, innovation, and wealth-producing potential when we raise our personal defenses. We then close out opportunities for discovering all the possibilities that exist. Closed, rigid attitudes atrophy and fail. Open, growing, and vital attitudes constantly reach new heights of formerly obscure possibilities.

Spirit and self-fulfillment.

To paraphrase Ralph Waldo Emerson: "What you are thunders so loudly that I cannot hear what you say." The state of our spirit conditions all of our attitudes and actions, even our appearance. The state of our souls is always expressed in our outer conditions and in the intangible influence that we radiate. My colleagues and I teach: "What you are *can* thunder so loud I'll *want* to hear what you say." The soul that is built upon a spiritual center shines out brightly through the life that it lives. Its mere presence heals and blesses all around it.

Self-actualization.

Mahatma Gandhi summarized the much discussed notion of self-actualization so beautifully and powerfully: "You will find yourself by losing yourself in service to your fellow man, your country, and your God."

This is the actualization of one's self. It is, of course, a beautiful way of expanding on the great truth that we sow what we reap. Zig Ziglar, a dedicated, motivated, and tough-minded man, says, "You can have everything you want in life if you will just help enough other people get what they want."

Recently, Zig and I were sharing the same platform as we addressed the National Speakers Association in Phoenix. He has to be one of the most self-actualized people I have ever met. I believe it would be virtually impossible for him to stand in front of an audience in a passive, plodding, and self-conscious way. He wants to give, stretch, and fulfill. His actions shout loudly that his life is actualized through service. The more effective a peak performer is, the more self-confident he or she becomes. The greater the self-confidence, the more likely its possessor is to be effective—to deliver total quality.

Instrumentation of intrinsic strengths.

Our weaknesses are only the absences of strengths. When you reach the rare condition of searching for, knowing, and relishing your strengths, you then find it relatively easy to look for, identify, and fulfill and unleash the strengths of others. This is the secret of one of the most powerful methods of empowering the possibilities of others.

Refuse to tolerate anything less than harmony in your life. You can have a happy and joyous life. But to do so you must seize the rudder of your own destiny and steer boldly for the port that you intend to make. What are you doing about discovering your true reality—the sum of your strengths?

Believing, behaving, and becoming.

What are you becoming? Perhaps there is no more urgent question for the manager in any enterprise to ask, especially those of us in our own aspiring TQC cultures. Remember, your example speaks more loudly than your words. It is your expectation of yourself that will determine your expectation of your job, your team members, your peers, and those who may be in higher positions. *It is your trust in yourself that determines how much you trust others. It is your love for yourself that determines your love for others.* In short, it is your input into life as a whole person that determines your love for others.

Investigate and install.

When you see a person who is delivering or achieving excellence, find out how and why. *Study excellence in every dimension of your life. If,* for instance, you are a salesperson and you've reached the point in your sales call where you are ready for an early or preliminary close, don't do it. It is crucial to go beyond this point and, through skilled and caring questions (ask, listen, and above all, hear) lead the other person to a new awareness of what can be! As one goes beyond just fulfilling newly determined wants and needs, the persuasive artist helps develop a new awareness of possibilities, and thereby solves much larger problems.

The gifted and wise parent learns to perceive strengths and possibilities in children by consistently looking for their uniqueness and then encourages, reinforces, guides, and leads them to an awareness and actualization of their possibilities way beyond the norm.

The same is true in business. If the original prospectors in South Africa had quit digging when they found a few diamonds in the yellow clay, vast diamond treasures would never have been discovered. It was only when a determined prospector dug all the way down to the blue clay that these riches were discovered. The possibilities revealed by persistent and consistent asking, listening, hearing, caring, and serving can open up whole new dimensions of richness for you and yours.

Love, light, and laughter.

What kind of people do you like to work with? Associate with? Sell to? Buy from? Gloomy, downbeat people invariably turn off, tune out, and exclude rich relationships in every dimension of their lives. If you believe, as I do, that we become what we think—we become what we expect—then expect to have love and laughter in your life. Laughter fueled by tough-minded love brings light into the darkest corners of human relationships and illuminates possibilities of the soul.

Itinerary.

The good life is one in which we are steadily moving toward clearly perceived dreams, ideals, and goals; we have a life itinerary. The old quote says, "Life is not a destination, but a continuing journey." A rocket can never get off the launching pad without fuel; a person can never begin and sustain a steady ascent toward dreams and goals without the fuel of faith, hope, love, and gratitude—synthesized and synergized by a progressive realization of our strengths. To continue the rocket metaphor, the successful rocket launch has an itinerary—a plotted trajectory and destination.

Tactics and tempo.

Every plan that is whole and complete consists of two major parts: strategy and tactics. Excellent strategic planning is rare, and is largely futile without closely reasoned and researched tactical planning.

Good tactical planning takes tempo into account: tempo is defined as *doing the right thing at the right time and in the right way.* The person who simply works long hours may not produce tempo and results. Activity by itself is meaningless!

Insincerity.

I have long been fond of the phrase "Phonies finish last." Insincerity kills dreams and defeats possibilities.

Excellence.

Excellence has such a beautiful and powerful ring. For over 35 years my colleagues and I have provided consulting and mentoring services to companies of all sizes. We have had the opportunity to serve 29 of the American companies cited in the book, *In Search of Excellence* by Tom Peters and Robert Waterman, Jr. It has been our privilege to help virtually all of them research, design, and develop a basic set of values that stress a culture of excellence and quality. When this wholesome and stretching set of principles and expectations pervades all of the policies, procedures, processes, programs, and people in the organization, the result is a significant escalation in profit and realized possibilities. A Total Quality Culture!

Salubriousness.

This word is used in a somewhat tongue-in-cheek sense. It smacks of joy—lightness, laughter, positive example, toughness of mind, ebullience, stretch, and strengths. Savor your uniqueness and resolve to confront the here-and-now challenge.

Armed with a positive philosophy, girded with principles, guided by practice, and sustained by faith, resolve to live life to its fullest. Walk tall, with the sure knowledge that the world needs and is hungry for the big, tough-minded individual. Will you do it?

PROFESSIONAL PLANNING FOR TQC WINNERS

I have recently spent time researching and thinking about the key differences between businesses that are adequate, good, and great.

Several elements emerge clearly. The most crucial element is planning. Planning, in the professional sense we are discussing here, is a dynamic blend of strategy and tactics that also includes provisions for excellent organization, coordination, expectation, and control.

At the very core of a total quality culture is a shared vision, with shared values and objectives in every dimension of the P-Pyramid, shown in Figure 3.

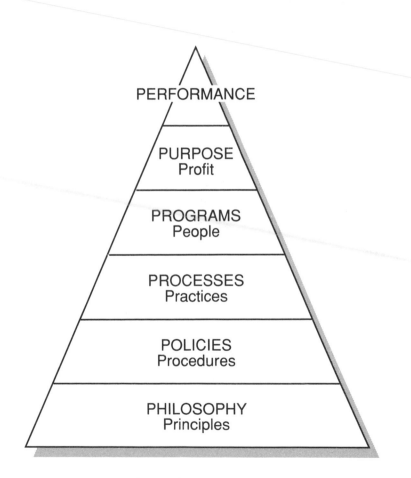

FIGURE 3.   The P-Pyramid

Real pervasive quality comes from having the elements of the P-Pyramid understood and applied at all levels in the organization.

My colleagues and I have never seen an enterprise become great without excellent planning. Here's how Harry Emerson Fosdick explained it: "No horse gets anywhere until he is harnessed. No steam or gas ever drives anything until it is confined. No Niagara is ever turned into light and power until it is tunneled. No life ever grows great until it is focused, dedicated, disciplined."

And James Russell Lowell puts planning into a hands-on perspective; "All the beautiful sentiments in the world weigh less than a single lovely action."

"Lovely actions" begin to happen when we exert discipline and dedication and make a plan. There are two key steps: Develop an orderly grouping of the basic beliefs and values that will be your philosophy in action. List several major result areas, often called key result areas or KRAs. These should be carefully shaped to the requirements of your particular business.

In order to achieve the optimum involvement and input from and by your team members, ask each of your TQC team to think through and write down the answer to each of the following questions. Do this thoughtfully yourself as well.

- Where are you now with regard to internal and external needs such as morale and competition?

- Capabilities and opportunities—what are they?

- Where do you want to go? List objectives and potentials.

- How are you going to do it? List policies, procedures and strategy.

- How are you going to accomplish your objectives? List programs, projects, and practices.

- What is your operational schedule? List objectives and programs in order of priority.

- Who will do what? Determine, clarify, and communicate the kind of organization, delegation, and developmental procedures you'll need.

- How will you pay? Determine your needs and budget these resources and describe their planned utilization.

- Why are you doing this? What do you expect to accomplish in terms of specific results, profitability and overall performance?

- How are you doing? Develop a concise, one-page (if possible) report that provides you with clear progress data on precisely how your business is doing in each of your key result areas (KRAs).

These involvement and input processes are essential to getting everybody involved so that when you ask for commitments, they will be carried out with conviction.

This no frills outline will give you a detailed approach to the specific nuts and bolts of planning and execution.

Even if much of this doesn't seem to apply to you now, please study it for use later on. You'll also find that sources of growth capital will be more apt to provide what you need when they see this type of planning and quality.

Anyone can provide rhetoric and hyperbole. But there is something about a thoroughly executed and disciplined plan that seems to say, "Here's a potential winner."

HOW TO MOTIVATE

"I can't seem to get myself in gear in the morning. I go to bed at night with rosy visions of what I'll accomplish tomorrow, but the next morning I seem to procrastinate. I get discouraged easily. Maybe I'm burned out."

"Maybe I'm burned out" has become a classical copout, a convenient and expedient reason to lay back and rest a little more. In reality, the number of cases of real emotional burnout, whatever that is exactly, are few. Close examination reveals such factors as:

- Lack of purpose. Failure to have something more important to live for than one's stomach and wallet.

- Insufficient self-esteem.

- Poor fitness habits: insufficient exercise, inadequate nutrition, excessive eating, drinking, or smoking.

- Blurred and indistinct expectations.

- Inadequate understanding of the renewing and revitalizing benefits of service. Few contemporary Americans understand what real service means—and the benefits to the server!

- A need to replace and displace a loser image of self with a winner image.

- Inadequate understanding of the renewing, toughening, strengthening, and enriching value of hard work when it is directed toward worthwhile and stretching dreams, goals, objectives, and specific action plans.

- The need for supportive and loving family, friends, and colleagues. It is not old-fashioned to believe that love is indeed a vitamin for the tough-minded that kindles vitality and quality.

- Lack of goals that require stretching and reaching.

These are some of the key factors that create a droopy face and extinguished eyes. When these deficiencies are handled, people begin to display contagious enthusiasm, sparkle, and glow. Let's look at a deficiency factor and discuss what can be done about it.

Insufficient self-esteem is at the core of most modern problems in every dimension of our society—in families, businesses, schools, and churches. There are a number of strategies that can be used to build self-esteem. One is to build a "strength notebook" in which you write down every strength you can think of about yourself, then add another every week.

I have known people who did not believe they could add an additional strength each week for even a month, yet they are doing it after three years.

As you become aware of your strengths, the benefits are enormous. First, you have more to offer those around you. You can only offer a cup of food to someone if you have first filled the cup. Become committed to this lifelong quest and life moves out of the shadows. It becomes joyful. People feel drawn to you. They want to be involved in things with you.

If you are a TQC leader who wants to move, grow, and build, buy or borrow from your library books on nutrition. Study them. Familiarize yourself with the materials of authorities like Dr. Carlton Fredericks, Dr. Emanual Cheraskin, Dr. Paavo Airola, Dr. Sam Walters, and Dr. Cass Igram. Check out physical conditioning facilities in your community and ask an authority to plan a complete fitness routine for you.

For spiritual fitness study the great religious writings. One of the most persuasive and successful businessmen I met told me he starts each day by repeating several times the Bible verse that says: "This is the day the Lord has made; I will rejoice and be glad in it."

This man never completed college, is not impressive to look at, and has a rather high voice. He said he had not accomplished anything significant until he began this daily practice. His fortune now is estimated to be over $2 billion and his family life is a model for most people.

BURNOUT IS CAUSED BY CONFUSION

Much of what passes for burnout is caused by the confusion we feel when we have not taken the time to think through and write down our expectations of ourselves and others, and our own personal conception of God. You need a *mission* that expresses a *vision* that the members of your team want so passionately that it calls forth their wholehearted commitment.

The need for a feeling of purpose greater than self cannot be over-emphasized. When we lead a life based only on self-aggrandizement and opportunism, we shrink as total persons. Growth stops, friends and associates fall away, and we consign ourselves to a narrow and frustrated future.

When we think, live, and work toward a dream or a grand design greater than ourselves, we stretch, reach, change, grow, and become enriched in every way. People want to associate with this kind of person.

Being Must Precede Doing

Jack Welch, CEO of General Electric says: "Over the past several years, we've wrestled at all levels with the question of *who we are* and what we want to *be*." This priority explains the new GE total quality culture and why GE is becoming one of the great companies for the 1990s.

LIST YOUR LIFE VICTORIES

If your career, indeed your entire life, is dedicated to exceeding yourself, you must understand the great lessons taught by leaders of history such as Christ, Churchill, and Gandhi, and by modern business executives such as Lee Iacocca, Ross Perot, Rich DeVoss, Art DeMoss, and others.

In every instance, they shared with their followers and associates the gift of a stretching dream—something to keep focusing on when daily or short-term adversities hit.

True self-motivation must be nourished and stimulated by a self-image that gives you a feeling of goodness, rightness, fitness, and—yes—*courage* to exceed your past and present self-image.

A tested and tough-minded technique for this is what we call the "200-victories commitment." Schedule some private time and write down 200 victories that you have achieved in your life. Believe me, you can list many more than 200. It seems difficult initially because many of us have allowed "loser" thoughts and sterotypes to dominate our minds and condition our self-image. Persist until you have actually written down your victories, beginning with the day you were born. The fact that you are alive is victory number one. You will notice a profound change taking place as you replace and displace loser thoughts, with winner thoughts . . . with *quality* thoughts.

Have this list typed neatly and continue to add "victories" as they occur to you. You'll find that you can do this once the initial transition from a losing attitude to a winning attitude has taken place. Remember:

> **When you truly see yourself
> as a winner—you become one.**

The word "work" appears in the Bible 564 times, and the great mystic Kahlil Gibran wrote in *The Prophet:*

> *Always you have been told that work is a curse and labor is a misfortune. But I say to you that when you work you fulfill a part of earth's furthest dream, assigned to you when that dream was born, and in keeping yourself in labor you are in truth loving life. And to live life through labor is to be intimate with life's inmost secret.*

The dynamic, tough-minded TQC leader will find that work is one of the finest, most pleasurable, and zestful ways available for building consistently high levels of self-motivation. There is something renewing and stimulating about knowing that you have a no-nonsense commitment to be achieved each day. You are committed to 100 percent quality.

Finally, there is no substitute for building relationships that are rooted in and fed by love with your family, friends, and colleagues. Such relationships consistently fuel us to do the un-doable; to reach beyond our grasp; to truly live, lead, and prosper.

The times cry out for people who dream big, plan big, and move forward with precision, skill, and confidence. Will you do it?

> *Our great and wonderful opportunity, however, is to chart a course of the* possible *dream and dare to keep our sight and senses on it. There may be setbacks and failures, but we will almost certainly have a higher level of accomplishment and actualization than if we have no dream at all.*

> —Joe Batten
> *Tough-Minded Leadership*

Chapter 4

Peak Performance at All Levels

Great coaches create a winning tradition on a foundation of vision, motivation, synergy, trust, respect, commitment, and attitude.

—Vincent H. Lombardi
Executive Excellence
April, 1992

America has produced a great many giants and a great many midgets. I've known giants who are four feet nine and midgets who are six feet six. It all depends on the size of one's character, one's attitude, commitment, care, dreams, and self-discipline.

Mary Lou Retton, Olympic gymnast and gold medalist, is admired throughout the world, and she is four feet nine inches of ebullient and joyful giant. The size of her commitment is awesome. Ross Perot is five feet six and a half inches and he is a *giant.*

John R. Noe's book *Peak Performance Principles for High Achievers,* (1989) is recommended for anyone who wishes a life of richness and great accomplishment. He closed this excellent story with these remarks:

> *What's the next high goal for Cindy and me? We'll keep climbing onward, since we have discovered the tremendous exhilaration that comes from living on the High Goals Cycle, sharing high achievements together, and constantly renewing our high goals in life. I hope this book has helped inspire you to set high goals and become a high achiever. When I end my seminars, I always close by saying, "May you have a good climb in your life and may you climb from peak to peak to the Peak, the Summit with God!"*

John Noe was a rather ordinary man for many years, until he decided to look for the best in himself and life. When he began to attempt to improve his physical condition, he could not run around the block without puffing and stopping. He was approaching middle age and was determined to truly live the rest of his life. He became a marathon runner and ultimately climbed the Matterhorn. Two years later, both he and his dauntless wife Cindy climbed Mount Kilimanjaro in Africa. They dare to scale the heights of their possibilities. Peak performers keep an eye on possibilities for reinventing themselves!

They dared to dream. Then they put muscles into those dreams. Here are five more nuggets from John:

1. It takes less energy to keep on climbing than to stop and hang on a ledge.

2. It takes less energy to go for the top than to wallow in the valleys of frustration and anguish.

3. It's easier to contribute to life than to lie around.

4. It's easier to grow than to decay.

5. It's easier to prepare than to procrastinate.

Peak performance is exhilarating and exciting! The moment you begin your preparation, you will experience tremendous energy, and each step will take you nearer to the ultimate accomplishment of your high goal.

Thomas J. Watson, long-time president of IBM, had a simple formula for achieving success: *Double your failure rate.* He knew that one crucial need in blasting your way out of the twilight of mediocrity was to dare mightily, to dip into your physical, mental, and spiritual reservoirs until that supply of strength has grown and grown. Muscle—whether physical, mental, or spiritual—can only grow if it is steadily tested and stressed. If you strap one arm to your side and give it total rest for three months, it will be atrophied, wasted, and weak. What does this tell us about the need for daily confrontation of our possibilities? For stretch and effort, for the need to keep reaching?

Abraham Lincoln was a so-called loser for many years. Take a look at what happened in the first 26 years of his adult career.

• 1832, lost his job and was defeated for the legislature.

• 1833, failed in business.

• 1835, lost his sweetheart to death.

• 1836, had a nervous breakdown.

- 1838, was defeated for speaker of Congress.
- 1843, was defeated in bid for Congress.
- 1848, was again defeated in bid for Congress.
- 1849, was rejected for land officer.
- 1854, was defeated for the Senate.
- 1856, lost nomination for Vice Presidency.
- 1858, was again defeated in Senate race.

He failed his way to success! He hung in there, consistently gave his best, and won the big one—the presidency of the United States.

Compare the philosophy and methods of Lee Iacocca, a modern tough-minded industrial "miracle man," as described in his autobiographical book, *Iacocca*, with the tough-minded words of Aristotle:

> *All men seek one goal; success or happiness. The only way to achieve true success is to express yourself completely in service to society. First, have a definite, clear, practical ideal—a goal, an objective. Second, have the necessary means to achieve your ends—wisdom, money, materials, and methods. Third, adjust your means to that end.*
>
> —Aristotle

As you put together your peak-performance tool kit, equip it with tested and timeless truths clothed in words and methods suitable for today and tomorrow. Note for instance how closely the great historian Arnold Toynbee has paraphrased Aristotle when he said: "First, an ideal which takes the imagination by storm, and second, a definite, intelligible plan for carrying that ideal into practice."

Based on years of counseling and mentoring with highly successful executives and leaders in some 80 percent of the Fortune 500 companies, as well as many small and medium-sized organizations, I submit that all really first-rate managers, leaders, and other peak performers have a great deal in common: *faith*. They believe deeply in the inspired thoughts that follow:

> *Make no little plans; they have no magic to stir men's blood and probably themselves will not be realized. Make big plans; aim high in hope and work, remembering that a noble, logical diagram once recorded will never die, but long after we*

are gone will be a living thing, asserting itself with ever-growing insistency.

—Daniel H. Burnham

Weak men are the slaves of what happens. Strong men are masters of what happens. Strong men are victors in any environment. Strong men may not change the circumstances, but they will use them, compel them to serve, and bend them to their purposes.

—George Craig Stewart

We often think of ourselves as living in a world which no longer has any unexplored frontiers. We speak of pioneering as a thing of the past. But in doing so we forget that the greatest adventure of all still challenges us—what Mr. Justice Adams called "the adventure of the human mind"! Men may be hemmed in geographically, but every generation stands on the frontier of the mind, in the world of ideas, there is always pioneering to be done, and it can be done by anyone who will use the equipment with which he is endowed. The great ideas belong to everyone.

—Mortimer J. Adler

Men grow when inspired by a high purpose; when contemplating vast horizons. The sacrifice of oneself is not very difficult for one burning with a passion for a great adventure.

—Alexis Carrel

I call that mind free which is not passively framed by outward circumstances, which is not swept away by the torrent of events, which is not the creature of accidental impulse, but which bends events to its own improvement, and acts from an inward spring, from immutable principles which it has deliberately espoused.

—William Ellery Channing

Peak performers do not paralyze themselves with obsessive worrying and self-criticism. They use doubt as a stimulus for a purposeful action.

—Charles Garfield

No horse gets anywhere until he is harnessed. No steam or gas ever gets anywhere until it is confined. No Niagara is ever turned into light and power until it is tunneled. No life ever grows great until it is focused, dedicated, disciplined.

—Harry Emerson Fosdick

The ultimate disease of our time is valuelessness.

—Abraham Lincoln

I know people who are antiques at 35, and others who can Watusi at 70.

—Maureen O'Sullivan

The quality of a person's life is in direct proportion to his commitment to excellence.

—Vincent Lombardi

I first met J. Paul Getty, the late billionaire, in 1968 when he was 75. One of the most memorable things he told me was that he loved to dance and considered himself excellent at doing the twist. I'd like to share some impressions and remarks of the man who was often described as the richest man in the world.

Most people who have read about him have assumed that earning money was his one consuming passion, and that he was not a joyful, healthy, and whole person. Nothing could be further from the truth. He radiated a positive attitude, fitness, and happiness. His interests were indeed broad and eclectic. In his delightful book *The Golden Age,* he places much emphasis on the need for a healthy, growing, and ever-changing mind, body, and spirit.

He has six chapters of financial and investment advice, but they are preceded by twelve chapters on how to prepare oneself broadly and deeply for full functioning as a person—how to savor life, to qualify as and be a connoisseur of the art of living. Getty knew that every age can be a golden age if one truly applies these tough-minded peak performance principles.

He prescribed this equation: Physical health + psychological preparation + activities and interests + gratifying human relationships − pernicious myths and misconceptions × an individual's energy and enthusiasm = the negation of age and triumphant 'connoisseurship of life' after retirement." You can:

> Discover your possibilities.
>
> Fulfill your potential.
>
> Actualize your dreams.
>
> Keep reaching and expect the best.
>
> Lead by example.
>
> Create your expective blueprint.
>
> Build on your strengths.
>
> Become what you think.
>
> Become what you say.
>
> Become what you expect.
>
> Focus on and commit to quality in every dimension of your life.

BUILDING TEAM VITALITY

Many analysts of current culture are examining what it takes for goals, attempts, beginnings, and good products to succeed. The magic doesn't seem to be there. After years of management, sales consulting, and leadership training, I have found that good intentions and fiery rhetoric won't do it. Self-starters must have vitality and voltage. Don't confuse this with high pressure, hype, and noise. They must reach, stretch, and empower.

We are discussing the kind of vitality that makes it both possible and desirable to:

- Do it.

- Do it right.

- Do it now.

- Do it right now.

In order to generate these practical qualities, we need to consider life-style and strength-building techniques.

First, life-styles need to include proper exercise, nutrition, rest, fulfilling achievements, and an attitude of mental toughness. It is beyond the scope of this article to detail methods of achieving optimum physical fitness, but it is clear that proper exercise and nutrition help vitalize the body and increase vitality. Without vitality, no TQC leader will grow or profit. The first thing to ensure is that your team understands the need for vitality and how they can attain it.

A second key ingredient for success is strength. Here is a process you can use to build strength for you and your team:

1. Seat your group in a circle not to exceed twenty people.

2. Each person writes down ten strengths they have identified in themselves.

3. Each person is then asked to look at each individual member of the group and mentally identify one significant strength in each person. No negatives of any kind are permitted.

4. Start at any point in the circle (with the first subject) and ask the person on his or her left to name one significant strength. Then proceed on around the circle until every person has informed the subject of his or her strength-oriented perception of that person.

5. Complete the total process and provide whatever guidance is needed to keep the remarks totally positive and strength-based.

You simply can't *build* anything from vacuum's, zeroes, and faults.

Many people, even of mature years, may hear for the first time about their strengths and receive affirmation and reassurance, which all of us are thirsty for.

Another important vitality and mental toughness bonus is that this is usually the first time each person has ever been asked to identify and articulate strengths—and only strengths—in anyone else. Special hands-on benefits of this process for a team include:

• Higher levels of confidence and self-esteem.

• New insights into the wants, needs, and possibilities of team members and clients.

• The growing capacity to resiliently spring back from disappointments and seeming setbacks.

• New feelings of commonality with other team members.

• Much greater capacity for long workdays and other manifestations of stamina. When your *every* thought, word, and action is primarily conditioned by a preoccupation with weaknesses rather than strengths, it literally saps and drains vitality. It makes true quality impossible!

Most "burnout" has little to do with overworked minds, bodies, and spirits; rather, it is primarily caused by boredom and a tendency to dwell on one's own weaknesses. Whenever we dwell on our weaknesses, we then tend to look for and relate to the weaknesses of everything and everybody around us. The creative benefits of strengths-building become obvious.

Recently I had the privilege of collaborating in some "seminars at sea" on a cruise ship with Ira Hayes, one of America's premier motivators, teachers, and speakers. Ira came all the way up through the ranks of the sales force at NCR without an advanced education. He is now in his sixties. But when Ira speaks—at huge rallies of up to 16,000 people or to intimate groups—his audiences listen and learn and laugh. He projects a special warmth that is eminently practical and effective. Why? The big secret is that Ira is convinced that life is great and the word *great* literally saturates his whole outlook, presentation, and actions.

His contribution to sales and leadership professionals has been enormous. Could he do this if he was bogged down in a preoccupation with his weaknesses—"can't," "don't," "won't," "didn't," "shouldn't," "wouldn't." You know the answer.

Charlie "Tremendous" Jones was originally just Charlie Jones—an ordinary guy. His success in insurance sales was mediocre. His level of vitality and voltage was "adequate." Then, as he began to discover the power of looking for all that was tremendous in everything and everybody around him, his sales volume began to move up and up until he became, while still a young man, one of the greatest insurance salesmen in America. He now devotes his life to helping people *see* how "tremendous" *they* can be. Charlie "Tremendous" Jones has *vitality* and *voltage*. He gets a lot done and has a lot of fun! And you can't do much of one without the other.

Some key factors, techniques, and considerations in effective team building include:

• Do sound and relevant research regarding wants, needs, and possibilities . . . in that order.

- Take time to define what you really want or expect to accomplish.

- Stress the right example.

- Allow for differences in the personalities, ambitions, and attitudinal set of team members.

- Develop consensus and unanimity.

- Provide steady feedback to provide progress data, recognition, feelings of team-belonging, and individual significance.

- Stress the importance of each team member learning to ask legitimate, caring questions.

- Be sure to teach and exemplify how infinitely more powerful a question is than a declarative statement in terms of practical persuasiveness.

- Ensure the mutuality of motives and expectations of all members of the team.

Finally, the excellent team needs *tempo,* defined as: *The speed with which an organization identifies problems and opportunities, and makes and implements decisions.*

For free enterprise to come into its own, we must practice and exemplify:

> Professionalism
> Commitment
> Vitality
> Focused strengths are the stuff of quality.
> Never-ending reaching and stretching.

THE STUFF OF EXCELLENCE

The magnificent possibilities in TQC will only reach their full potential when the components of excellence are understood and practiced. For over 30 years, my colleagues and I at The Batten Group have taught the understanding and hands-on implementation of this concept.

Some quotes and examples follow which have been tested—they are the tools for the 90's. In 1972 my daughter Gail and I wrote *The Confidence Chasm* (Batten and Pedersen). Here is what we said in a subsection entitled, "The Search for Excellence":

In the process he learned to respect himself, which is necessary fuel for the continuous pursuit of excellence. Aristotle said, "Lose yourself in productive work—in a way of excellence.". . . Jesus said, "Ask, and it shall be given you; seek, and you will find; knock, and it shall be opened to you." The great men expected much from themselves and from other people, in that order . . . individuals committed to excellence.

All these men have based their philosophy on knowledge of one's capabilities through confrontation, on respect for self and love of others, and on the importance of building a solid foundation of values to live by—in short, the pursuit of excellence—demonstrating in the process why they were happy people in the real sense of the word.

With regard to the Biblical question. "Am I my brother's keeper?" we said, "Rather, we ought to play the much tougher role of 'brother's brother' and help him to *keep himself*—in other words, be true to the way of excellence."

Please accompany me on a vicarious trip as Gail and I share with you the abbreviated story of what happened in a company that turned it all around—that moved from mediocrity to excellence:

As all the various "P's" in the organization were reviewed— philosophy, policies, procedures, practices, principles, processes, privileges—the company's bulletin boards, staff meetings, house organ, and other methods of in-house communication were thoroughly overhauled. The employees began to receive a message of high expectations, or emphasis on excellence and quality. They were told in every way possible that the company's concern for their individual dignity and worth would be reflected in new procedures designed to compensate them only for results, only for the demonstrated use of their full abilities as quality team members.

This change from a permissive climate to one of high expectations was in no sense accomplished overnight. The first months brought no great degree of mutual satisfaction.

By the end of approximately three years, however, there had been a discernible increase in the beat and tempo (always a key indicator of excellence) of activity, in individual pride of of achievement, and in the prevailing respect for dignity and worth of both employees and management.

The drab history of this company also included the fact that a number of young M.B.A.s recruited into the management development program had departed after a few months or, at best, two or three years. A searching examination revealed that a principal reason for this was that each young recruit felt that he or she was being *cared for* rather than challenged. That he or she was being given something he or she had not earned. That he or she was not going to have to reach into their inner resources and find new strengths and new talents and a new ability to cope.

The management development program was accordingly revised so that it reflected, both in its in-house operations and in its campus-recruiting aspects, a better approach. A *tough and demanding set of standards*, the potential executive was informed, would be "applied with great consistency once he became a member of the company." The most crucial change, however, was that management began to stress (and practice) this need for positive, enlightened leadership by example and to set an *example of excellence*.

Interestingly, many of the young people who had previously applied for positions with this company had represented a type which no longer showed up in the university placement offices for interviews. They were prescreened by the tough-minded and demanding criteria listed as preconditions for employment. They preferred not to stretch, not to grow by continually confronting unfamiliar situations and difficulties. The young people who replaced them were as tough as the exacting standards they welcomed; they were eager to discover new strengths, new abilities within. Make no mistake about it, there are many of these tough-minded young people. But *few can demonstrate these attributes in the absence of sufficiently high expectations.*

Expect More from Your Team—And You'll Get It

A number of years ago, I met in Atlantic City with management development executives from IBM divisions around the world. The objective was to further develop and implement tough-minded practices to achieve excellence. After spending a number of stretching hours with these dynamic and creative people, we wrote:

> *So simple and yet so tough. So simple and yet so powerful. One of the major reasons for IBM's particularly great success is the fact that the fundamental foundation of the organization cuts right to the heart of the human condition—to the need for significance, the need for identification with something bigger than self, the need to respect oneself before one can respect others. By great service, we build not only abundance of the pocketbook, but abundance and actualization of the spirit. Profitable? Decide for yourself.*
>
> *—Batten and Pedersen, 1972*

Entrepreneurs may be asking, "What does all this have to do with me? With quality?" My answer would be: Everything! Mature management and marketing concepts and practices are urgently needed by those entrepreneurs who want to reap the rewards of excellence with *total* quality.

I particularly recommend the book *Peak Performers,* by Charles Garfield. His first-rate research and writing has provided some excellent and nostalgic affirmation for me. When Leonard Hudson and I wrote *Dare to Live Passionately* (1966), our statement that the key to a great life was "passionate commitment to a transcendent mission" was figuratively received with yawns. We were asked, "What does *passion* have to do with management?

When Charles Garfield told me of the impact this particular statement had on his life, I was very gratified. His role in presenting the efficacy of passion over passivity in building a quality culture is significant.

Chapter 5

Winners Can Be Grown

Stimulate and relish change. Don't be frightened or paralyzed by it. See change as opportunity, not just a threat.

—John F Welch, Jr.
CEO, General Electric

Do you think and talk like a winner? Do you have a winner's expectations?

Did you know that the terms *peak performer, total quality,* and *winner* all mean the same?

I recently had the pleasure and privilege of speaking for several hours to the sales force of one of the most successful companies in the world. They had experimented with a strategy for growth and development that had produced profound results—a bottom line that crackled and glowed.

For a number of years, they told me, they had been using my books, tapes, and films and were particularly intrigued and challenged by the following three concepts:

- We become what we think.
- We become what we expect.
- We become what we say.

The notion that we become what we say is not found in the literature or vocabulary of business in general. But this company was intrigued and committed themselves to the following:

> All members of the organization are expected to study, master,
> and apply the following "tough-minded terms" to every facet
> of operations.

The terms that follow are a partial listing, with definitions, of these terms for all who are committed to TQC as one of the finest possible ways to live, work, and create wealth in our free enterprise system. A more complete list of tough-minded terms is given in the glossary at the end of this book.

A Westinghouse computer expert who attended one of my seminars once told me that he had researched the tough-minded/expective materials and had found 374 terms whose definitions were different and much more stretching and positive than the conversational and written norm. Ross Perot says there are over 400.

Here, then, are over 40 tough-minded terms. Please study them, and question, experiment with, and apply these power concepts. They have been taught in over 100 cities annually by Batten Seminars. These terms are at the very core of TQC.

Activity. Sound and motion that signify nothing unless they culminate in a targeted result. Things that one does.

Aggressiveness. Initiative that is primarily self-serving. Not to be confused with assertiveness, which uses one's strengths for purposes of building.

Analyze. To divide the whole into its component parts (who. what, where, when, how, why) in order to determine the nature, proportion, function, and relationship between the parts. Often not productive unless followed up by *evaluation, synthesis,* and *synergy.*

Assertiveness. The vulnerable exposition of strengths. Since strengths are all we possess, and thus are all we have to assert, vulnerability permits the full use of these strengths without defensiveness.

Climate. The temperature of the human environment in which one finds oneself; the "feel," the "chemistry," more often sensed than known. The sum of the attitudes in an organization. Positive climates can literally produce marvels and miracles. The "feel" and "sense" of the company's culture.

Coach. To help others develop insights and actions in order to achieve mutually understood goals. This pertains particularly to helping one identify, surface, fuse, and focus one's present and potential strengths and expectations.

Commitment. An internalized, then externalized, concentration of desire and energy focused on various degrees of achievement. An "integrity of intent." An unshakable commitment of energy regardless of adversity.

Communicate. Moves beyond dialogue (two or more people engaged in monologues). Builds on strengths, openness, and open listening, and results in shared meaning and understanding.

Confront. To openly, honestly, and vulnerably address that which needs to be addressed. The reverse of expedience, obliqueness, deviousness, or avoidance.

Cybernetic. From the Greek word *kybernetes,* meaning "steersman." A self-correcting system whose function is perpetuated by a closed loop or servomechanism. The human being is the finest cybernetic unit in the world.

Develop. To generate, synthesize, nurture and ultimately create something better.

Directive. Words or actions, felt or implied, that arbitrarily indicate a desired action or result. Tends to suggest compression and pushing rather than evoking and stretching (as in expective).

Discipline. Training and development that builds, molds, and strengthens; lean, clean, focused behavior.

Emotional context. A blend of emotions such as anger, fear, disgust, grief, joy, and surprise to achieve learning or modification of behavior. A blend relationship between two people in a business environment seldom results in much real learning.

Empathy. The imaginative projection of one's consciousness into the consciousness of others. Put yourself in the other person's place. This is an indication of maturity, regardless of chronological age.

Evaluate. To identify the relative value of a person, place, thing, or relationship; the values or strengths revealed by the analysis.

Expectation. A desire, want, or need communicated in the form of a clear request. The ultimate gift, it says to others, "I value and appreciate your possibilities."

Goal. Something one wishes to accomplish. Broader and more timeless than an objective. Expressed as a desired and targeted happening.

Hard. Rigid, compressed, repressed, suppressed, depressed, oppressed, brittle, dead, weak. The reverse of toughness. Hard things crumble under stress. Tough things resiliently endure.

Individual. In the tough-minded vocabulary, this term means the opposite of a rebel. Rebels live, talk, and work in terms of what they are *against;* individuals live, talk and work in terms of what they are *for.* A rebel dissents. An individual protests.

Loyalty. A quality or action of steadfastly adhering to one's beliefs in a person or thing by every thought, word, or action. You must give loyalty in order to receive it.

Management process. In the tough-minded management lexicon, this means the following sequence: research, vision or mission, plan, organize, coordinate, execute, control.

Motivation. Motive-action: "action to achieve motive." First motives (results, objectives, goals) are developed, and then action plans are designed to accomplish them.

Open listening. Truly open "hearing" with heart, mind and soul. A felt and expressed desire to truly understand the other person.

Organization. Means "organ in action." In business, government, and other kinds of endeavors, it is the collective functioning of a group to achieve missions, goals, and objectives. For maximum effectiveness it requires the "logical and creative deployment of strengths."

Passive. Yielding, quiescent, nonresponsive, with a low level of reaction. The "bland leading the bland." Avoids living at the cutting edge of life. Reacts rather than proacts. "Laid back."

Philosophy. A body of truths and firm beliefs. Organizationally, it is the basis for the development of mission, goals, objectives, organization, expective action plans, and controls. The basic beliefs and values that fuel and guide both organizations and individual lives.

Plan. An orderly assortment of actions designed to fulfill a mission or accomplish a goal or objective. An objective by itself is not a plan. It is only the basis for one. It consists of two key elements: strategy and tactics.

Responsibility. Response-ability or "ability to respond." Responding fully to the pledge of a commitment; responding in a manner consistent with full integrity.

Results. The final happening. Not to be confused with a measurement of a result. The reason for all activity.

Self-confidence. The belief that you are significant, unique, and good. A growing awareness of one's own strengths, often with a heightened zest for strong, testing, and confrontive challenges.

Self-discipline. The commitment of oneself—in discipleship—to worthwhile courses of action or programs of development and fitness. Usually such commitment transcends self-interest.

Significance. The feeling that a person "counts," is real, and is accomplishing good stretching, and relevant things in life.

Strength. The true realities in all things. Conversely, weaknesses are only what is absent or lacking. Strengths are the only building blocks in anything, the only resources one can employ in every dimension of life. The meaning of *strength* and *integrity* is the same.

Synergy. Since all that goes up must ultimately converge, synergy is the magnified impact of a confluence or synthesis of strengths. In synergy, 2 + 2 = 5 or even more. The whole is greater than the sum of the parts. The real meaning of teamwork.

Team. A combination of people, or other productive units, working in dynamic and positive conjunction with one another to produce synergistic results. A group that shares a common toughness of mind.

Tool. A useable resource or combination of resources to accomplish a desired level of achievement. Something one usually employs directly to get something done. Our *real* tools are our individual strengths.

Tough-minded. An open, growing, changing, questing, stretching, *quality* of mind. Characterized by tenacity, resilience, flexibility, durability, and suppleness. The qualities on which the future of the world depends. Most problems stem from a hard, rigid, insecure mind.

Trust. The feeling that expectations will be met. The implicit belief in the integrity, or strength, of the potential behavior of another person.

Value. The intrinsic worth or strength of anything. It should be preceded by analysis and is identified by evaluation.

Vital. Bursting with life and positively directed energy.

Vulnerable. Openness to experience. An affirmation of belief in the essential goodness and rightness of life. The absence of defensive, petty, or suspicious behavior. *Vulnerability* and *confrontation* are closely related. Vulnerable people grow. Invulnerable people close up and atrophy.

Warmth. Emotion and caring, flowing toward others, that transmits feelings of affirmation, reassurance, and love. Overt evidence of a desire to build and give to another, reflected in tone of voice, facial expression, and the free expression of positive emotion.

"We" feeling. This occurs when one particularly enjoys the practice of giving earned praise to others and when commitment to the goals of the organization transcends personal wants, needs, and problems. Reflected in speech by the use of "we" instead of "I." The feeling that one is part of a hard-hitting team that gets results. This feeling is possible only when people feel like individuals—with individual purposes, values, and dignity focused on a common goal.

Wisdom. The ability or gift of transcendent vision. To see the "big picture," to visualize the immediate need or problem in proper perspective. A knowledge of fundamental truths and the ability to use them in a meaningful, developmental, and positive way, producing a course of action that achieves desired results.

Wonder. The ability to perceive that which is fresh, vital, and good in all people and all things. The most practical and wonderful lives are crafted and lived by wonder-full people.

Your future in your TQC role and in life itself depends on how you fuel, test, and stretch your mind, your attitude, by wonder-full thoughts and actions. You truly become what you say. Think and speak like a winner and you become one. Will you do it?

THE ANATOMY OF WINNING

"Everything I try fails! When I look in the mirror it isn't very pleasant because I see a loser there. Joe, do you really believe what you were just saying—that *anyone* can be a winner?"

This question is all too familiar. I'm asked this time after time after serving as a mentor in an organization or as I step down from the speaking platform.

This question deserves a thoughtful answer. First, it is important to make a distinction between "being" and "doing." Action that isn't coordinated by the right kind of mental preparation can lead to failure. For instance, do you remember the old verse that says:

> A centipede was happy quite,
> Until a frog in fun
> Said, "Pray, which leg comes after which?"
> This raised her mind to such a pitch,
> She lay distracted in a ditch
> Considering how to run.

The centipede should have had a clear working knowledge of *who* and *what* it was before doing. "Being" must precede "doing."

The key to being a winner is to develop clarity about your purpose, direction, expectations, and priorities. I have seen countless lives changed for the better when the person clarified, organized, and targeted his or her attitudes. Emmett Fox, the great metaphysical clergyman said: "Some years ago I coined the phrase 'mental equivalent.' For anything you want in your life—a healthy body, a satisfactory vocation, friends, opportunities, and above all the understanding of God—you must furnish the mental equivalent. . . . The secret of successful living is to build up the mental equivalent that you want; and to get rid of, to expunge, the mental equivalent that you do not want."

The power of the mind—particularly the tough mind fueled by a tender heart—is awesome. It is estimated that the average human brain contains 287,000 times the computative units in the most advanced computer. To learn more about its potential, a world-famous psychiatric and psychological research center has been studying the human brain for many years. The researchers found that the brain of the "average" person utilized only six to eight percent of its cells during his or her entire life.

It is also alleged that the brain of the late and brilliant Albert Einstein had only utilized some 9 to 11 percent of its capability during his distinguished lifetime.

Ask for What You Want

There is a famous Bible verse that forms the acronym ASK:

> **A**sk and it will be given you.
>   **S**eek and you will find.
>   **K**nock and it will be opened unto you. (Matthew 7:7)

Note that each of these statements is a duality: each has expectation and reward, and each is an expective and a result.

Now, study and restudy the following 16 elements. I have named them the Circle of Quality Living.

• Know what you can and will expect from yourself.

- Let yourself perceive all of your possibilities.
- Determine specific components of your dream.
- Decide the what, where, when, who, how, and why of what you want to be and do.
- Determine how well the goals can and must be realized.
- Schedule, prioritize, develop your "life calendar."
- Apply your mind and skills diligently.
- Believe in yourself, in others, and in God. Believe others are right unless proven wrong.
- Believe in your expectations.
- Remember that love is the central source of energy that makes it all happen.
- Gratitude is the highest form of mental and spiritual health.
- Let life in. Seek, quest, appreciate, enjoy.
- Dissolve your emotional defenses.
- Savor the flavor of each passing moment.
- Caring, sharing, and forgiveness are a sure guarantee of growth, change, and fulfillment.
- *Asking* is the finest way to express all of the other portions of the circle—to actualize one's quality possibilities.

There is another powerful technique that I used with a man who came to see me. He said he could no longer find or hold a job. He wanted me to arrange a job interview for him.

I agreed on one condition. He would first have to prepare a list of 200 victories in his life, starting from the time he was born. The list had to be in his own handwriting, and I had to be satisfied that he had prepared it with no help from anyone else. If he did this, I would arrange a job interview.

He came back three days later with only 40 victories and informed me that he couldn't think of any more. I reiterated firmly that he must meet my terms or no job appointment.

At the end of 10 days he returned, and he had somehow managed to complete the 200 victories. His complexion looked better and he already moved with a bit more bounce. He had met the terms of the agreement, but I also asked him to do the following:

Follow modern tested recommendations for sound nutrition and begin vitamin and mineral supplements.
Visit a dentist for a thorough dental overhaul.
Visit a barber.
Begin a planned daily regimen of physical workouts.
Listen to my tape *The Greatest Secret* 20 times.

Then I arranged the interview, and he was hired. Today he holds a major executive position in a fine company. What is the message here? He replaced and displaced negative thoughts with "victorious" or "winner" thoughts. I asked him to continue to add victories to his list, and he now tells me that it is easy. He thinks like a winner! He has made the transition from loser to winner with the aid of a healthier body and—above all—the aid of a mind fueled and strengthened by power values.

Years ago there was a commercial that said, "Life is swell when you keep well." Here is a modern equivalent: "Life is a joy when you think like a winner." Will you do it?

FOUR WINNING TRAITS

Do you like to sit and watch the action from the sidelines? If so, there is a logical and good place for you.

Or do you enjoy the thrill of being in the arena doing it yourself? If so, there is a place for you, too.

One of the great things about our free enterprise society is that there is a place for *every* person who holds sincere beliefs and practices them.

One of the things all aspiring TQC leaders should realize is that whether a person likes the action of the arena or prefers to sit on the sideline and watch—it doesn't matter. Remember, the race and prizes do not go only to the swift or the aggressive. One cannot profile an ideal personality trait profile in order to predict who will be a successful TQC practitioner. Rather, we should recognize that there are a battery of human qualities that cut across all personality types and pervade all levels of successful TQC leadership.

For many years my colleagues and I have constructed and presented courses on selling, leadership, and management. Our experience has shown that the most potent elements of all of those programs can be represented by four words: *share, care, dare,* and *be aware.*

Sharing

When we meet with our teams—we meet in a basement, a hotel or motel, an office suite, or a school or church recreation room—there are important principles to remember if we are to communicate in ways that build prosperity, organization, and pleasure. To communicate at the high level at which we genuinely share ourselves, it is important that we:

- Avoid presentations. Invite every kind of question, comment, anecdote, experience, suggestion, and recommendation.

- Listen. Get behind the person's facial expression and sense what they really want and need and mean.

- Be vulnerable. If there is even a smidgeon of defensiveness in your voice, words, manner, and posture, you will probably turn someone off. You'll never know why, and perhaps they won't know either.

- Avoid slick, highly literate, highly articulate methods of "pitching." A pitch-person practically never makes it big in a valid and fine company. If you study the qualities of those who are great successes, you find people who are:

  —down to earth

  —frank and open

  —interested

  —thorough and meticulous in followthrough

  In short, turn the word "tell" around so that it becomes "let," and cultivate the practical art of letting others in and letting *you* out.

Caring

One of the legendary names in selling was the late Frank Bettger author of *How I Raised Myself from Failure to Success Through Selling* (1991). Frank and I spoke to an audience of several thousand salespeople in Atlanta one evening, and I learned at dinner that he was 79 years old. When he was on stage, I was fascinated to hear him speak for two and a half hours with no notes or podium. He held the audience spellbound as he shared selling and persuasive techniques with them.

His dedication to the audience was unmistakable. They felt this, and gave him a standing ovation. The next day in the Atlanta airport, I asked him how he could do this. His answer said it all. "Before I walk out on the stage, I concentrate on what my experience tells me they need and I just *share* everything I can give them. I try to always remember that 'go-getters' are a dime a dozen. If you *give* your all, you'll always *get* more.

How do you become a consistent "sharing pro"? The answer: you must care enough. When you care about every dimension of life and let it show, amazing things happen. Here are some specific ways to reflect caring in your present and future relationships:

- Give thought to comfort, convenience, and timing when you arrange appointments or meetings with those whose lives can be enriched by an affiliation with you.

- Make sure your knowledge of your product, methods of operation, compensation, and suggested actions is thoroughly studied, thought through, and correct.

- Build on strengths; don't dwell on weaknesses.

- Share humor, laughter, and upbeat thoughts.

- Make that extra phone call or drop that extra note that says you care.

- Give them one of the finest gifts—the gift of clear expectations based on your assessment of their strengths.

- Reflect, by example, that the words "serve and "sell" mean exactly the same.

- Care enough to write down details about the features and benefits of every proposed project. Be sure copies reach all appropriate people.

Dare to Be Aware

Burt Reynolds, in an interview with *Success* magazine some months ago, said, "Macho is garbage—vulnerability is everything." The real Burt is anything but a macho guy. His friends and associates describe him as thoughtful, caring, easy to talk to, sensitive, and helpful. The times cry out for people who are strong and confident enough, man or woman enough, to shed the outdated macho and machismo wrappings like a snake leaves his skin behind in the spring.

Superior cultures are of, by, about, and for people who care enough to share. They are aware of the wonders, uniqueness, strengths, and possibilities of everyone with whom they associate. They enjoy helping others fulfill their highest values and become all they can be.

These people are at a premium. We need more of them. Do you care, share, and dare enough to be aware of the infinite possibilities just waiting to be discovered in others? I'm going to bet that you do.

Tomorrow's Culture

There go my people; I must follow them, for I am their leader.

This bit of whimsy carries the seed of a dangerous and pervasive half-truth that can blur the real nature of leadership.

Most of our current leadership vocabulary is dated. I maintain that the following phrases are oxymoronic—self-canceling terms:

Directive-leadership
Values-*driven* leadership
Running an organization

As we have seen, leadership and top quality don't exist without followers. And followers are not driven; they are pulled. They are not pushed: they are led! They are not diminished; they are enhanced!

Do *you* feel:

Pushed by your values or *led*?
Pushed by your motives or *led*?
Driven by your vision or *pulled*?
Driven by data or equipped to *reach*?

Do you feel more stimulated and responsive when:

> You are *told* rather than *asked*?
> You are *compressed* rather than stretched?
> You are *running* rather than *leading* an operation?
> Your *weaknesses* are *emphasized* and your *strengths* ignored.

Are your vision and values *behind* you . . . *pushing* you? Or are your vision and values ahead of you . . . *pulling* you? Charles Garfield (1986) says, "No matter which measure of worth predominates in any given person, when all else is said and done, the force with the strongest *pull* toward high achievement concerns quality, principle, intrinsic value."

What would happen to a spacecraft that had tremendous thrust, but no orbit or trajectory plotted? What happens to your team members if you give them lots of push, thrust, and pressure without clear and stretching expectations and guidelines? The answer is pretty obvious.

People often respond that these are only words, only semantics, and how important are *words*? In actuality, we ultimately become what we say! Words are the only tools we possess. How can computer software be developed without words? What can fax machines transmit that is not created by, interpreted by, and acted on except words? How can lasers be created and used without words? How can new concepts of quality be created with words? Here is a preliminary list of truly *expective* leadership words and their *directive* or *driven* counterparts.

Expective Words

Expect. To look forward; to anticipate; to consider probable or certain.

Elicit. To call forth or bring out a response, to draw forth; to evoke; to bring out something latent.

Motivation. Motive-action; action guided and pulled by motive-action to achieve motive; motive-led.

Directive Words

Direct. To impel an authoritative instrument forward.

Drive or Driven. Having a compulsive or urgent quality; applying force to push.

Congest. To concentrate in a small or narrow space; to become congested.

Expective Words

Pull. A force that attracts, compels, or influences; magnetic force; to seek to obtain by making one's wants known. To call on for a response.

Ask. To call for; to seek; to invite; to make a request.

Stretch. To extend in length; to pull taut; reach or continue from one point to another; search for a better way.

Leader. A first or principal performer of a group. To be in front; to lift, guide, expect, empower, communicate, and achieve results.

Directive Words

Push. A physical force steadily applied in a direction away from the body exerting it.

Tell. To give utterance to; to assure emphatically.

Compress. To reduce in size or volume as if by squeezing; flatten; to make inert.

Stereotyped "leader". Drives and congests; practices warmed-over "management" methods

Ever try to *push* a shoestring?
Now *pull* it and see what happens.

THE CHOICE IS OURS

Individuals, relationships, and groups that open and stretch *grow*. Individuals, relationships, and groups that close and shrink *die*. A follower is defined as "one who follows the opinions or teachings of another; one who imitates another." It is crucial that followers clearly perceive and understand the ideas, dreams, and goals of the leaders. These visions and objectives can only be communicated by words. Your effectiveness will rise or fall in direct proportion to your word usage and skills. Words can make your team members feel pushed, crowded, and even guilty. Conversely, words can make us feel lifted, stretched, and exhilarated.

Some key words and phrases for the tough-minded leadership lexicon include:

Expect	Stretch	Release
Ask	Listen	Hear
Customer-led	Market-led	Possibilities
Request	Expand	Renewal
Elicit	Enhance	Empowerment
Evoke	Unfold	Empathic
Lift	Blossom	Build
Compete	Care	Coach
(with self)	Communication	Confront (one's
Commitment	Warmth	possibilities)
Consistency	Vision	Vulnerability
Vitality	Serve	(emotional)
Resilient	Significance	Value-led
Responsibility	Strength bank	Positive stress
Symbiosis	Possibility teams	Synergy
Quality	Excellence	Respect
Love	Counsel (not	Passion
Help	advise)	Integrity

The creative deployment of strengths.

Strengths enhancement.

Performance is all that matters.

Attitude is everything.

A system of expective leadership.

Reverse the G-forces.

Relish and embrace change.

Above all—integrity.

We are transformed by the renewal of our minds.

Learn, learn, learn.

OUR MOST PRICELESS GIFT

We human beings are walking bundles of blessings and possibilities, and the world in which we live provides vastly more opportunities for growth, change, and enrichment than we can perceive.

The greatest gift of all is the ability and opportunity to learn! We must constantly alter our paradigms, our visions, our values, and what we are becoming. Central to the Total Quality Culture is the opportunity to share learning so that all group activity is synergistic. The great corporations of tomorrow will, above all, be *learning corporations*. They will consistently move toward a culture that provides alignment, creativity, and empowerment (ACE).

THE JAPANESE EDGE

"We have been striving to be the Picassos and Beethoven of electronics."

—Akio Morita, CEO
Sony Corporation

Since my last trip to Japan, I am constantly asked what the Japanese know that we don't and what they're doing that we aren't. It sounds simplistic, but here it is:

1. We still *know* more than they do.

2. They are, however, *demonstrating* and *practicing* three things that many of our quick-fix, one-minute executives seem to have forgotten. These are:

    —Self-discipline and structure
    —Focused and intensive commitment to stretching visions
    —Energy and hard work

Their enthusiasm for the new tough-minded Total Quality Culture paradigm was palpable. Their eagerness to *learn* these things is currently unmatched in America. Richard Lesher, president of the United States Chamber of Commerce, says: "Those countries (Europe and Japan) have fairly rigid institutions, but we are very flexible. Combine the TQM discipline with our adaptability, and you can predict the results with certainty." I agree. We can do it!

THE ESSENCE OF THE TQC PARADIGM: SUMMING UP

1. A tough-minded leader provides transcendent or macro vision and magnetic lift and pull, like a compass. The science of physics would probably not exist without the magnetism of particles. A tough-minded leader provides purpose and direction.

   RESULT: Quality

2. A tough-minded leader provides a crystal-clear focus of all strengths in the organization. Knowing that our strengths are our tools, a tough-minded TQC leader expects and reinforces the best.

   RESULT: Quality

3. A tough-minded leader is committed to *people, service, innovation, team building* and *quality.* A TQC leader believes this commitment is liberating and enriching to all.

   RESULT: Quality

4. A tough-minded TQC leader leads by an example that is focused stretching and positive. A leader is motive-led and value-fed. Nothing communicates quite like example.

   RESULT: Quality

5. A tough-minded TQC leader ensures that all compensation is related to positive performance and expects total integrity. A leader is guided in all decisions by these two components.

   RESULT: Quality

The problem is not the competitor (the Japanese). The problem, the challenge, is the person in the mirror. And the solution is the person in the mirror.

Will you adopt the positive values that lead to success?
Will you lead your colleagues to do the same?
Will you dare to stop pushing and driving, and say "Follow me"?

THE RESULT: Quality!

Appendix A _____

QUALITY AFFIRMATIONS FOR THE TQC LEADER

I will exemplify a passion for excellence.

I will ask, listen, and *hear*—to determine the wants, needs, and possibilities of my customers and my team.

I will provide an example of accountability, commitment, and integrity.

I will follow a path of continual empowerment for myself and others.

I will consistently look for a focus on the strengths rather than the weaknesses of all with whom I come in contact.

I will cultivate optimum physical, mental, and spiritual fitness.

I will lead as I would like to be led.

I will savor the flavor of each passing moment.

I will enfuse every thought and relationship with faith, hope, love, and gratitude.

Appendix B

A TOTAL QUALITY CULTURE MISSION STATEMENT

> The mission of this company is to create a culture in which the search for the highest quality is incessant, and the lessons learned are similarly implemented in every dimension of the organization.
>
> All rewards will be based on how well this commitment is fulfilled.

Bibliography

QUALITY WITHOUT TEARS, Philip B. Crosby (New York: McGraw-Hill 1984)

PEAK PERFORMERS, Charles Garfield (New York: Morrow, 1986)

TOP PERFORMANCE, Zig Ziglar (New York: Berkley Books, 1990)

THE LEADER'S EDGE, Bert Nanus (Chicago: Comtemporary Books, 1990)

THE MAKING OF THE ACHIEVER, Allen Cox (New York: Rodd, Mead and Company, 1984)

ORGANIZATIONAL CULTURE AND LEADERSHIP, Edgar H. Schein (San Francisco: Jossey-Bass, 1985)

THE RENEWAL FACTOR, Robert H. Waterman, Jr. (New York: Bantam Books, 1987)

EXCELLENCE IN LEADERSHIP, Frank Goble (New York: AMACOM, 1972)

CORPORATE CULTURE, Terence E. Deal and Allan A. Kennedy (Reading, Mass: Addison-Wesley, 1982)

AMERICAN SPIRIT: VISIONS OF A NEW CORPORATE CULTURE, Lawrence M. Miller (New York: Morrow, 1984)

LEADERS, Warren Bennis and Burt Nanus (New York: Harper & Row, 1985)

LEADERSHIP, James M. Burns (New York: Harper & Row, 1985)

DEVELOPING A TOUGH-MINDED CLIMATE FOR RESULTS, Joe Batten (New York: American Management Association)

TOUGH-MINDED MANAGEMENT, Joe Batten (3rd edition, 1978) (New York, American Management Association)

TOUGH-MINDED LEADERSHIP, Joe Batten (New York: AMACOM, 1989)

TOUGH-MINDED PARENTING, Joe Batten (Nashville: Broadman Press, 1991)

WHEN GIANTS LEARN TO DANCE, Rosabeth Moss Kanter (New York: Simon & Schuster, 1990)

LEADERSHIP IS AN ART, Max DePree (New York: Doubleday, 1990)

HOW TO BE HAPPIER IN THE JOB YOU SOMETIMES CAN'T STAND, Ross West (Nashville: Broadman Press, 1991)

THE CORPORATION OF THE 1990's, Micbael S. Scott Morton (New York: Oxford University Press, 1991)

THE LEADERSHIP CHALLENGE, James M. Kouzes and Barry Z. Posner (San Francisco: Jossey-Bass, 1987)

SUPER LEADERSHIP, Charles C. Manz & Henry P. Sims (New York: Prentice-Hall Press, 1989)

MANAGING THE FUTURE, Robert B. Tucker (New York: G.P. Putnam & Sons, 1991)

THE ART OF THE LEADER, William C. Cohen (New York: Prentice-Hall, 1990)

EXPECTATIONS AND POSSIBILITIES, Joe Batten (Santa Monica: Hay House, 1990)

PEAK PERFORMANCE PRINCIPLES FOR HIGH ACHIEVERS, John R. Noe (New York: Berkley Publishers, 1989)

Glossary

Accountability. The "ability to account" for the extent to which a commitment is met.

Action Plan. A sequenced and prioritized chronology of intent, commitment, and tactics; what one is going to get done and some of the key activities involved.

Activity. Sound and motion that signify nothing unless they culminate in a targeted result. Things that one does.

Aggressiveness. Initiative that is primarily self-serving. Not to be confused with assertiveness, which uses one's strengths for purposes of building.

Amateur or obsolete competitor. To compete with others rather than with one's own self-generated goals. One who seeks to beat or defeat another person or group.

Analyze. To divide the whole into its component parts (who, what, where, when, how, why) in order to determine the nature, proportion, function, and relationship between the parts.

Appraisal. To determine the value and possibilities implicit in a person's performance and personality at a particular time.

Assertiveness. The vulnerable exposure of strengths. Since strengths are all we possess, and thus are all we have to assert, vulnerability permits the full use of these strengths without defensiveness.

Build. The blending of strengths into a composite whole. Key elements in tough-minded team building are those in which the team is armed with a positive *philosophy,* guided with *principles,* guided by *practices,* and sustained by *faith.*

Builder. The CEO who stands tall is, above all, a builder. Committed to vision, stretch, empowerment, synergy, responsiveness, flexibility—toughness of mind—a builder ensures that all dimensions of each P in the pyramid are intensely focused on creation, growth, and building.

Candor. Applied truth. In the tough-minded lexicon, this involves openness, emotional vulnerability, awareness of the needs of others, and a genuine desire to build them up.

Caring. Consistent manisfestation of concern for and affirmation of others. The perception that all people are right until proved wrong and that each person is a bundle of strengths and possibilties.

Climate. The temperature of the human environment in which one finds oneself; the "feel," the "chemistry," more often sensed than known.

Climate for mistakes. An environment that calls for and reinforces constant experimentation, creativity, innovation, and change. Encourages the practice of "failing forward." Mistakes within reason are rewarded rather than penalized.

Coach. To help others develop insights and actions in order to achieve mutually understood goals. This pertains particularly to helping one identify, sufrace, fuse, and focus one's present and potential strengths and expectations.

Collaboration. Coordination in action. A blend of strengths to produce positive sybiosis and synergy.

Commitment. An internalized, then externalized, concentration of desire and energy focused on various degrees of achievement. An "integrity of intent."

Communicate. Moves beyond dialogue (two or more people engaged in monologues). Builds on strengths, openness, and open listening, and results in shared meaning and understanding.

Communication. Shared meaning; shared understanding.

Compensation. Providing or receiving full value, psychological or financial, for energy expended in accomplishing results.

Confront. To openly, honestly, and vulnerably address that which needs to be addressed. The reverse of expedience, obliqueness, deviousness, or avoidance.

Consistency. Consonance of unity of thought, word, or deed over a continuum of time, space, or relationship.

Consultive decision making. A decision-making process in which the leader involves team members and secures their best input prior to making any major decisions. The tough-minded leader places a premium on asking, listening, and hearing. Thus, when he or she makes a decision and stresses the logical deployment of strengths, team members are expected to meet lean, stretching commitments. Clear-cut accountability is a crucial operational requirement here.

Control. An end result of interactive processes involving clarity of expectation and the achievement thereof. Control is not a tool per se. It is a result of excellence in applying the other concepts in the tough-minded leadership system.

Conviction. Individual and team evidence of strong persuasion; the manner in which strong commitment, fueled by involvement, is practiced; fulfillment of a pledge.

Coordinate. To share meaning and understanding in order to permit and require the synchronized effort of appropriate people to achieve mutually understood goals.

Counsel. See **coach.** They are tightly related.

Criticize. To evaluate the results of analyses and identify the values or strengths therein. To build on those strengths in seeking to improve the situation, person, or thing.

Culture. The pervasive philosophy, central values, beliefs, attitudes, and practices of an organization, and the micro-elements that make things happen.

Customer-led automated marketing system (CLAMS). A total operational system fed by imaginatively programmed touch-screen computers to provide constant and comprehensive customer input as a basis for ongoing evaluation and improvement of the entire P-pyramid.

Cybernetic. (From the Greek word *kybernetes,* meaning steersman.) A self-correcting system whose function is perpetuated by a closed loop or servomechanism.

Develop. To generate, synthesize, nurture, and ultimately create something better.

Dignity. The worth, significance, and uniqueness of a person; an awareness of intrinsic worth. Clear, consistent expectations and a constant search for and focus on strengths affirm this dignity.

Directive. Words or actions, felt or implied, that arbitrarily indicate a desired action or result. Tends to suggest compression and pushing rather than evoking and stretching (as in **expective**).

Discipline. Training and development that builds, molds, and strengthens; lean, clean, focused behavior.

Dissatisfaction. A preoccupation with past failures; a tendency to dwell on what didn't work. On the contrary, *un*satisfaction is a healthy, hungry desire to change, grow, and move onward and upward.

Doubt your doubts. To consistently and responsively subject one's doubts to positive analysis and evaluation to determine latent possibilities.

Dream. A deeply felt hope of the possible. Dreams lift and move individuals and organizations to the highest level.

Emotional conflict. A blend of emotions needed to ensure that knowledge or information is transmuted and transmitted into learning. A *gestalt* of feelings.

Emotional context. A blend of emotions such as anger, fear, disgust, grief, joy, and surprise to achieve learning or modification of behavior. A bland relationship between two people in a business environment seldom results in much real learning.

Empathy. The imaginative projection of one's consciousness into the consciousness of others. The ability to put yourself in the other person's shoes.

Empower. To create and foster relationships in which people understand their significance, possibilities, and strengths. People who are empowered have a clear understanding of their authority, responsibility, accountability, and valued role in the team, and they have autonomy that is symbiotic with others. You get power by giving power.

Evaluate. To identify the relative value of a person, place, thing, or relationship; the values or strengths revealed by the analysis.

Excellence. What happens when you give an undertaking your best shot and know it.

Exemplar. Leaders whose personas and actions represent the essence of what they say and expect.

Expectation. A desire, want, or need communicated in the form of a clear request. The ultimate gift, it says to others, "I value and appreciate your possibilities."

Expective. A more specific statement of expectation; a clear oral or written request. As contrasted with a directive, it is designed to stretch rather than to compress, to pull rather than to push.

Faith. Belief in and commitment to causes, quests, and affirmations that transcend self-concern.

Feedback. Information that clearly indicates the progress and corrective needs of the ongoing project or undertaking.

Flexibility and resilience. The opposite of rigidity. The living and committed responsiveness to possibilities, difficulties, and opportunities.

Focus. A point at which energy converges. Concentrated centering of effort. A focused team shares these perceptions and acts accordingly.

Forgiveness. A requisite for growth, happiness, and exponential renewal. As we develop a life-style that is based on being "for-giving" rather than being "for-getting", we become capable of forgiving.

Free enterprise. Freedom of individual action to chart and accomplish a full measure of individual achievement—economically, politically, socially, and spiritually; freedom to develop the whole and apply full talents to stretching work assignments.

Fully functioning team. The reverse of a dysfunctional team. A team that epitomizes and validates the tough-minded principles in action. A group that consistently meets, surpasses, and develops new dimensions of goal actualization.

Gestalt. A structure in which the response of a person or an organism to a situation is a complete whole rather than simply the sum of the parts or elements; a total configuration of factors.

G-forces. The figurative pull of gravity. Negative G-forces of the past are passive, self-defeating attitudes, and practices that retard and even reverse growth and forward movement. Positive G-forces of the future are passionate attitudes and practices that help pull and guide the leader to move toward the future in the most productive, energetic, and positively magnetic way. Like a compass, positive G-forces guide and pull.

Goal. Something one wishes to accomplish. Broader and more timeless than an objective. Expressed as a desired and targeted happening.

Go-giver. A positive term replacing the cliché "go-getter"; a tough-minded person who knows that one can achieve much more when major energies are directed toward giving encouragement, knowledge, inspiration, and understanding to others rather than seeking self-aggrandizement only.

Grace. A special warmth felt and expressed toward all other human beings; an absence of pettiness and self-concern. A living manifestation of the belief that a person should devote major energies to doing something *for* others and not *to* others.

Gratitude. Thoughts, feelings, and actions that reflect and transmit appreciation and earned praise.

Hard. Rigid, compressed, repressed, suppressed, depressed, oppressed, brittle, dead, weak. The reverse of toughness.

Incident file. A document in which key episodes (both positive and negative) are recorded. To be used for developmental coaching and counseling.

Individual. In the tough-minded vocabulary, this term means the opposite of a rebel. Rebels live, talk, and work in terms of what they are against; individuals live, talk, and work in terms of what they are for.

Innovation. Newness in action. Ever-searching, ever-changing concepts, methods, research, and application.

Integrity. Strength, reality, authenticity, toughness.

Interdependent. Reciprocal interaction of mutually dependent team members. Such interaction becomes synergistic when the individual team members are provided (equipped) with feelings of significance, constant learning, positive values and examples, focus, and clear expectations.

Intuitive leadership. The demonstrated capacity to take correct actions without necessarily knowing why. Accurate guesses, whether educated or merely sensed. A feel, a sense, a sensation in the gut of what is appropriate. Quick and ready insight.

Involvement. Joint and shared use of talents to develop, clarify, and achieve symbiotic relationships and synergistic results.

Job description. A listing of key result requirements that constitute or define a job or position.

Judge. To form subjective conclusions about another. Judgments project our negative feelings about ourselves into others; they are a projection of weaknesses. The reverse of **evaluate.**

Key result areas. Major areas of an individual's position or job. They are usually determined so that objectives or standards will be established for all significant responsibilities of the position. Term may also be used to apply to a major emphasis of an enterprise or project.

Kinesics. "Body English." The study of body movements, facial expressions, and so on as ways of communicating.

Lead. To be in front, figuratively. To lift, guide, expect, empower, communicate, and achieve synergistic results.

Leadership. The exercise of a system of expectations; an everchanging, ever-dynamic gestalt of interacting minds, designed to mobilize and maximize the most effective use of strengths to achieve objectives.

Leadership by expectation. Leadership in which a complete and pervasive system of expectations is established throughout the organization and is fueled by the logical deployment of strengths. Leadership by expectation involves the belief that people are the alpha and omega of all organizational success. Such a leader practices virtually all the principles and methods in this book.

Leadership by renewal. The consistent practice of the principles and methods in this book with primacy given to the belief that all team members are more productive and actualized when they are reaching, growing, involved, empowered, and discovering new feelings of individual significance. It is a tough-minded axiom that a leader must first become this kind of person in order to provide true leadership by renewal.

Love. A feeling of brotherhood and good will toward other people. Tough-minded leaders express love via a disciplined committment to build rather than to destroy—to enhance rather than to diminish—all associates and team members through every thought, word, and action. Although it is an ideal, the TML seeks to build this emphasis on enhancement pervasively throughout the organization's *P-Pyramid*.

Loyalty. A quality or action of steadfastly adhering to one's beliefs in a person or thing by every thought, word, or action.

Management by objectives. A management style where, all decisions and actions are executed for the purpose of achieving and exceeding clearly defined and agreed-upon objectives.

Management process. In the tough-minded management lexicon, this means the following sequence: research, vision or mission, plan, organize, coordinate, execute, control.

Mission. A stretching, guiding, and reinforcing statement of intent and commitment.

Motivation. Motive-action; "action to achieve motive." First motives (results, objectives, goals) are developed, and then action plans are designed to accomplish them.

Motive power. Focused and positive use of energy to achieve a motive or motives. One's personal motor, which enables one to reach and fulfill a motive.

Negative. Any action that involves retreating from the challenge and discipline required to achieve positive results.

Nice guy. One who is affected, self-deprecating, insincere, overly subtle; hence, evasive and untrustworthy. Used in this context to mean a person who chooses the easier alternative and rationalizes this action with "nice" clichés. One who retreats from the requirements of demanding self-discipline.

Nurture. To provide insights, expectations, reinforcement, asking, listening, and hearing that grow people.

Objective. Something one wants to get done. A specific statement of quality, quantity, and time values.

Open listening. Truly open hearing with heart, mind, and soul. A felt and expressed desire to truly understand the other person.

Organization. "Organ in action." In business, government, and other kinds of endeavors, the collective functioning of a group to achieve mission, goals, and objectives.

Organize. To blend resources logistically to achieve objectives; to deploy strengths logically.

Passion. Intense, focused feelings fed in synchromeshed conjunction by the value system described in this book.

Passive. Yielding, quiescent, nonresponsive, with a low level of reaction. The "bland leading the bland."

Performance. Discernible and productive actions moving beyond target or intent and actually fulfilling a commitment.

Performance standards. A baseline level of achievement. Commonly defined in the literature as "A standard indicates performance is satisfactory when. . ." Meeting standard performance is the basic requirement for maintaining a position. Extra rewards should be bestowed only when the standard is exceeded.

Philosophy. A body of truths and firm beliefs. Organizationally, it is the basis for the development of mission, goals, objectives, organization, expective action plans, and controls.

Plan. An orderly assortment of actions designed to fulfill a mission or accomplish a goal or objective. An objective by itself is not a plan; it is only the basis for one. It consists of two key elements: strategy and tactics.

Positive stress. The opposite of negative stress, which causes dissonant disaster and distress; positive stress is healthy, intensely focused energy applied to positive goals.

Possibility team. A dynamic group of people to blend strengths to discover, recommend, and achieve innovative improvement in all dimensions of the organization.

Power. Qualities emanating from the leader that exert compass-like pull, both subtle and overt. Such qualities provide both direction and attraction, purpose and pull. Positive, forward-focused influence.

Power teams. A team that is lifted and stretched toward new and exciting levels of positive achievement. A team that is value-centered and value-led.

P-Pyramid. The pyramidal triangle that presents the following sequence of Ps: philosophy (principles), policies (programs), procedures (processes), practices (projects), and profit (purpose). These Ps represent the complete infrastructure of any organization.

Presence. A total appearance or impression projected by an individual, which emanates confidence and effectiveness and inspires the confidence of others.

Purpose. An overriding, lifting, stretching end to be attained.

Quality. The degree of excellence a thing possesses. Also see **total quality.**

Rebel. A person who knows, and is primarily motivated by, what he or she is against; to know what one is against and be motivated accordingly. See also **individual.**

Renewal. Innovation and renovation. The process of making fresh, strong, and good; new physical, mental, and spiritual strength.

Renewal organization. The type of organization in which all the Ps with emphasis on the people are geared toward the practice of the principles described in this book.

Respect. Feelings, felt and expressed, that reflect enhanced awareness of the dignity, worth, and individuality of another person.

Responsibility. Response-ability, or "ability to respond." Responding fully to the pledge of a commitment; responding in a manner consistent with full integrity.

Result. The final happening. Not to be confused with a measurement of a result. The reason for all activity.

Rigid thermometer. A descriptive term for a person whose attitudes and actions simply register the temperature of the climate in which one functions.

Self-actualized. Focused, activated, and fueled by the entire value system described in this book with particular emphasis on clarity of expectations, building on strengths, and enhancement and empowerment of the team. The self-actualized leader lives and works within the context of a transcendent vision of the possible.

Self-confidence. The belief that you are significant, unique and good. A growing awareness of one's own strengths, often with a heightened zest for strong, testing and confrontive challenges.

Self-discipline. Commitment of oneself—in discipleship—to worthwhile courses of action or programs of development and fitness. Usually such commitment transcends self-interest.

Self-esteem. (See **self-confidence**). Esteem is, perhaps, a more immediate and *now* sense of confidence.

Self-led teams. Where focus, commitment, and follow-through are generated from within the team. The synergistic conjunction of motivated individual members of the team.

Service. The ongoing product of a passionate commitment to fulfill the wants, needs, and possibilities of others.

Servosystem. A closed-loop cybernetic process that provides for macro-organizational feedback and responsiveness as well as micro-individual feedback and responsiveness. Such macro and micro servosystems will make possible the kind of responsiveness to customers that must shape the volatile leadership wave of tomorrow.

Significance. The feeling that a person "counts," is real, and is accomplishing good, stretching, and relevant things in life.

Social gestalt. A dynamic interweaving of individual behavior patterns that produces group accomplishment greater than the sum of its parts.

Sophisticated. Artificial, highly complicated, refined; maintaining a facade that obscures the basic truths of the situation.

Strategy. A careful plan or method focused on macro goals. Completed, fulfilled, and sometimes exceeded with the aid of tough-minded tactics; micro-focused action steps.

Strengths. The true realities in all things. Conversely, weaknesses are only what is absent or lacking. Strengths are the only building blocks in anything, the only resources one can employ in every dimension of life. The meaning of *strength* and *integrity* is closely related.

Strengths bank. A computerized database containing the salient strengths of all relevant personnel. This bank is accessed regularly to truly practice the logical deployment of strengths. All major assignments are made and decisions are conditioned by such deployment. Since strengths are indeed the only reality in a person, the strengths bank enables an organization to move forward on the basis of total reality. Weaknesses are regarded merely as missing strengths or insufficiently developed strengths.

Stress. See **positive stress.**

Stretch. A questing, reaching search for a better way.

Symbiosis. A relationship where living or working together provides and enhances mutual advantage.

Synergy. Since all that goes up must ultimately converge, synergy is the magnified impact of a confluence or synthesis of strengths. In synergy, $2 + 2 = 5$ or even more. The whole is greater than the sum of the parts.

Synthesize. To combine an individual's values and strengths discovered during an evaluation.

System. Dynamic, reciprocating aggregate of sequenced actions to achieve properly determined objectives.

System of values. A complete and functionally compatible combination of essential truths. Values are the subjective interpretation of the immutable laws of the universe that shape and guide human reactions. The orderly expression and transfer of tough-minded values into practices is the essential process involved in building a climate of productivity.

Team. A combination of people or other productive units, working in dynamic and positive conjunction with one another to produce synergistic results. A group that shares a common toughness of mind.

Team development. To elicit and evolve possibilities for internally generated growth. To identify, unify, and synergize individual strengths. Thus, a whole greater than the sum of its parts.

Teaming. An ongoing process; a leading-edge example of all of the "we" factors in action.

Team motivation. Motive power in action, expressed synergistically. A tough-minded blend of pull (goals) and push (accountability).

Team synergy. Shared meaning, values, beliefs, strengths, commitment, stretch, and reward.

Tenacity. Resilience, staying power, ability to bounce back. Determination to prevail through thick and thin. Focused endurance.

Theory X. A management style described by Douglas McGregor in *The Human Side of Enterprise.* It illustrates the reverse of all that is advocated in this book by stressing the use of organizational rank and directiveness as one's first expedient.

Theory Y. Another management style created by Douglas McGregor. It places a premium on caring about people and empowering them to give their best efforts to team accomplishment. It is in general agreement with tough-minded leadership (TML).

Theory Z. A management style described in William Ouchi's book *Theory Z,* it is based on thirteen steps practiced by leading Japanese companies. This approach derives from numerous applications of tough-minded management techniques initially introduced to Japanese businesspeople by Konosuke Matsushita, then chairman of the board of Matsushita Industries. He has credited Batten, Batten, Hudson and Swab, Inc. as the source of these seminal techniques.

Tomorrow-mindedness. An approach in which all the Ps in the P-Pyramid of an organization are designed and instrumented to anticipate, create, and innovate to meet requirements of the future. A tomorrow-minded leader is responsive rather than reactive.

Tool. A usuable resource or combination of resources to accomplish a desirable level of achievement. Something one usually employs directly to get something done. Our real tools are our individual strengths.

Total quality. Integrity of function and composition.

Total Quality Culture (TQC). Concentrating all people and resources on a never-ending quest for greater quality in *every* dimension of the culture of the organization. Beyond Total Quality *Management* (TQM), TQC is *pervasive.*

Tough. The integrity of a substance, person, place, thing, or feeling. Characterized by tenacity, resilience, flexibility, durability, and suppleness.

Tough mind and tender heart. A synergistic blend of attitudes and actions that reflect stretch, tenacity, discipline, warmth, and caring.

Tough-minded. Open, resilient, growing, changing, questing, stretching quality of mind. Having an infinite capacity for growth and change. See **tough** and **tough-minded leader.**

Tough-minded competitors. Those that consistently confront their possibilities, compete with their own self-generated goals, and constantly seek to *become all they can be.*

Tough-minded leader. The kind of leader who, much like a compass, provides direction and, figuratively, magnetic pull. The TML "walks in front of the flock," and exemplifies the system of values and practices that this book is all about.

Tough-minded thermostat. A descriptive term for a person whose attitudes, commitment and actions *change* the temperature of the climate in which they function.

Tough-minded toolbox. Our strengths are our tools! This toolbox sits on the shoulders of the person, and the efficacy and effectiveness of these instruments grow in direct relationship to one's commitment to continuously searching for new strengths and their application.

Trust. The feeling that expectations will be met. The implicit belief in the integrity or strength of the potential behavior of another person.

Unity. Oneness of purpose, focus, communication, and action.

Unsatisfaction. A healthy and hungry desire for new growth, new effectiveness, new levels of achievement. The reverse of **dissatisfaction.**

Valuability. Ability to value; ability to ascribe value to an event, circumstance, object, or person, and *act.* Subjective interpretation and response—as in response-ability or responsibility.

Value. The intrinsic worth or strength of anything. See **system of values.**

Value-Added. A product or service to which have been added features and benefits to delight the customer.

Value system. A dynamic, reciprocating, and reinforcing conjunction of values.

Vision. A transcendent view of the possible.

Visioneering. Having vision fed by a synergistic blend of resources tooled for achievement. The term we use to describe the tough-minded leader's kit of tools for the future.

Vital. Bursting with life and positively directed energy.

Vulnerable. Openness to experience. Affirmation of belief in the essential goodness and rightness of life. The absence of defensive, petty, or suspicious behavior.

Warmth. Emotion and caring, flowing toward others, that transmits feelings of affirmation, reassurance, and love. Overt evidence of a desire to build and give to another, reflected in tone of voice, facial expression, and the free expression of positive emotion.

"We" feeling. This occurs when one particularly enjoys the practice of giving earned praise to others and when commitment to the goals of the organization transcends personal wants, needs, and problems. Reflected in speech by the use of "we" instead of "I." The feeling that one is part of a hard-hitting team that gets results. This feeling is possible only when people feel like individuals—with individual purposes, values, and dignity—focused on a common goal.

Wisdom. The ability or gift of transcendent vision. To see the "big picture," to visualize the immediate need or problem in proper perspective. A knowledge of fundamental truths and the ability to use them in a meaningful, developmental, and positive way, producing a course of action that achieves desired results.

Wonder. The ability to perceive that which is fresh, vital, and good in all people and all things. The most practical and wonderful lives are crafted and lived by wonder-full people.

Yeast. A volatile blend of organic substances that creates synergistic growth. The "good bacteria" are the organizational components treated in this book. The "bad bacteria" are the components of directiveness, expedience, rigidity, and other elements of style that will not meet the requirements of a turbulent tomorrow.

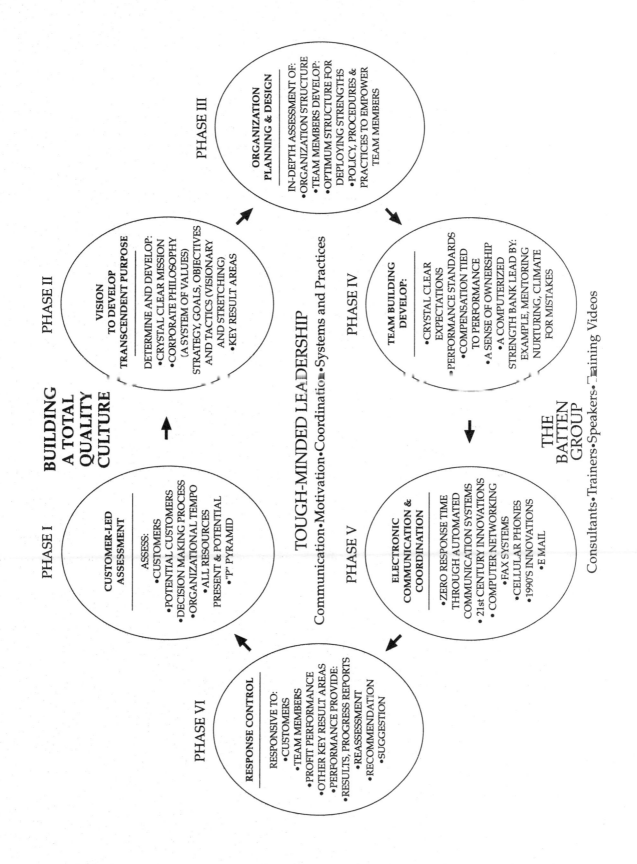

BUILDING A TOTAL QUALITY CULTURE

TOUGH-MINDED LEADERSHIP
Communication•Motivation•Coordination•Systems and Practices

PHASE I

CUSTOMER-LED ASSESSMENT

ASSESS:
- CUSTOMERS
- POTENTIAL CUSTOMERS
- DECISION MAKING PROCESS
- ORGANIZATIONAL TEMPO
- ALL RESOURCES PRESENT & POTENTIAL
- "P" PYRAMID

PHASE II

VISION TO DEVELOP TRANSCENDENT PURPOSE

DETERMINE AND DEVELOP:
- CRYSTAL CLEAR MISSION
- CORPORATE PHILOSOPHY (A SYSTEM OF VALUES)
- STRATEGY, GOALS, OBJECTIVES AND TACTICS (VISIONARY AND STRETCHING)
- KEY RESULT AREAS

PHASE III

ORGANIZATION PLANNING & DESIGN

IN-DEPTH ASSESSMENT OF:
- ORGANIZATION STRUCTURE
- TEAM MEMBERS DEVELOP:
- OPTIMUM STRUCTURE FOR DEPLOYING STRENGTHS
- POLICY, PROCEDURES & PRACTICES TO EMPOWER TEAM MEMBERS

PHASE IV

TEAM BUILDING DEVELOP:

- CRYSTAL CLEAR EXPECTATIONS
- PERFORMANCE STANDARDS
- COMPENSATION TIED TO PERFORMANCE
- A SENSE OF OWNERSHIP
- A COMPUTERIZED STRENGTH BANK LEAD BY: EXAMPLE, MENTORING NURTURING, CLIMATE FOR MISTAKES

PHASE V

ELECTRONIC COMMUNICATION & COORDINATION

- ZERO RESPONSE TIME THROUGH AUTOMATED COMMUNICATION SYSTEMS
- 21st CENTURY INNOVATIONS
- COMPUTER NETWORKING
- FAX SYSTEMS
- CELLULAR PHONES
- 1990'S INNOVATIONS
- E MAIL

PHASE VI

RESPONSE CONTROL

RESPONSIVE TO:
- CUSTOMERS
- TEAM MEMBERS
- PROFIT PERFORMANCE
- OTHER KEY RESULT AREAS
- PERFORMANCE PROVIDE:
- RESULTS, PROGRESS REPORTS
- REASSESSMENT
- RECOMMENDATION
- SUGGESTION

THE BATTEN GROUP
Consultants•Trainers•Speakers•Training Videos

RECOMMENDED VIEWING FROM

THE BATTEN GROUP
2413 Grand Avenue
Des Moines, IA 50312

JOE BATTEN VIDEOS

Tough-Minded Leadership
Keep Reaching
When Commitments Aren't Met
Solving Employee Conflict
Power-Packed Selling: The Trust Factor in Customer Relationships
The Face-to-Face Payoff, Dynamics of the Interview
The Nuts and Bolts of Performance Appraisal
I Understand—You Understand: The Dynamics of Transactional
    Analysis
The ABCs of Decision Making
A Recipe for Results: Making Management by Objectives Work
No-Nonsense Delegation
The Nuts and Bolts of Health-Care Management Communication
Tough-Minded Interpersonal Communication for Law Enforcement
Evaluating the Performance of Law Enforcement Personnel
Creating a Tough-Minded Culture
Tough-Minded Supervision for Law Enforcement
Commitment Pays Off
Friendly Persuasion
Keep on Reaching
Trust Your Team
Dare to Dream

JOE BATTEN FILMS/VIDEOS

Ask For the Order and Get It (Dartnell-Chicago, Illinois)
Your Price is Right, Sell It (Dartnell)
Manage Your Time to Build Your Territory (Dartnell)
When You're Turned Down . . . Turn On (Dartnell)
Your Sales Presentation . . . Make It a Winner (Dartnell)
Management by Example (BNA—Rockville, Maryland)
The Man in the Mirror (BNA)
The Fully Functioning Individual (BNA)
The Fully Functioning Organization (BNA)
The Fully Functioning Society (BNA)

RECOMMENDED LISTENING

AUDIO CASSETTES

How to Apply the Tough-Minded, Decision-Making Process
The Nuts and Bolts of Health Care Management Communication
Tough-Minded Supervision for Law Enforcement
How to Install a Tough-Minded Performance Appraisal System
Joe Batten on Management
The Greatest Secret
Face-to-Face Motivation
Face-to-Face Management
Secrets of Tough-Minded Winners
How to Exceed Yourself